CONSTITUTIONAL

PATRIOTISM

CONSTITUTIONAL
PATRIOTISM

Jan-Werner Müller

PRINCETON UNIVERSITY PRESS

PRINCETON AND OXFORD

COPYRIGHT © 2007 BY PRINCETON UNIVERSITY PRESS

PUBLISHED BY PRINCETON UNIVERSITY PRESS, 41 WILLIAM STREET,

PRINCETON, NEW JERSEY 08540

IN THE UNITED KINGDOM: PRINCETON UNIVERSITY PRESS,

3 MARKET PLACE,

WOODSTOCK, OXFORDSHIRE OX20 1SY

Library of Congress Cataloging-in-Publication Data

Müller, Jan-Warner, 1970–

Constitutional patriotism / Jan-Werner Müller.

p.   cm.

Includes index.

ISBN 978-0-691-11859-8 (hardcover : alk. paper)

1. Citizenship. 2. Citizenship—European Union countries. 3. Patriotism.

4. Patriotism—European Union countries. I. Title.

JF801.M85   2007

323.6'5—dc22   2007004766

BRITISH LIBRARY CATALOGING-IN-PUBLICATION DATA IS AVAILABLE

THIS BOOK HAS BEEN COMPOSED IN JANSON

PRINTED ON ACID-FREE PAPER.

PRESS.PRINCETON.EDU

PRINTED IN THE UNITED STATES OF AMERICA

1 3 5 7 9 10 8 6 4 2

. . . der Gedanke, der den Wunsch, seinen Vater, tötet,
wird von der Rache der Dummheit ereilt.

—Theodor W. Adorno, *Minima Moralia*, no. 79

CONTENTS

CONSTITUTIONAL

PATRIOTISM

INTRODUCTION

"CONSTITUTIONAL PATRIOTISM": the expression will sound in many ears like a contradiction in terms. Constitutions serve, by definition, to limit political power and to render power impersonal; patriotism is about mobilizing men and women for personal political sacrifice. Constitutions are, for the most part, settlements that emerged from interest-based bargains, they are the "autobiography of power";[1] while patriotism, on the other hand, makes an appeal to transcend self-interest. Constitutions, ideally, articulate not just norms and wider social aspirations, they also protect individual rights; patriotism, however, tempts citizens with illiberal forms of "group-meaningfulness" (George Kateb) and can make them ride roughshod over civil rights and liberties.[2] Perhaps it's true that patriotism, as Alasdair MacIntyre once put it, "turns out to be a permanent source of moral danger." Or it might even be the case that, as Kateb has claimed, "patriotism is inherently disposed to disregard morality."[3]

"Constitutional patriotism"—as understood by those who originally put forward the idea and as understood in this essay—designates the idea that political attachment ought to center on the norms, the values and, more indirectly, the procedures of a liberal democratic constitution. Put differently, political allegiance is owed primarily neither to a national culture, as proponents of liberal nationalism have claimed, nor to "the worldwide community of human beings," as, for instance, Martha Nussbaum's conception of cosmopolitanism has it.[4] Constitutional patriotism offers a vision distinct from both nationalism and cosmopolitanism, but also from republican patriotism as traditionally understood in, broadly speaking, the history of Euro-American political thought.

The idea of constitutional patriotism has enjoyed very varying fortunes so far. It was born in post-war, divided Germany and has often been seen as a poor substitute for a "proper" national identity—a substitute that was to become redundant after the country's unification. Yet constitutional patriotism has experienced a major renaissance since the mid-1990s when observers both inside and outside Germany began to view it as a normatively attractive form of civic, non-national (or perhaps even post-national) attachment for increasingly multicultural societies.

In recent years, the idea has also been advanced as a way of conceptualizing "civic identification" at the supranational level, with some scholars explicitly calling for a "European constitutional patriotism."[5] Why would such a thing be necessary? A common response goes like this: the process of European integration has remarkably sped up during the 1980s and especially the 1990s; this rapid "deepening," together with the continuous enlargement of the European Union (EU), has led to much agonized thinking about what could "hold Europe together." While politicians, scholars and citizens continue widely to disagree about the exact nature of what a former President of the European Commission, Jacques Delors, once called an "unidentified political object," only few dispute that the EU now faces an increasing gap between what Michael Walzer terms "moral" and "legal communities."[6] The legal community of the Union is stretching from the Canary

Islands to the Eastern border of Poland; from Malta to Lapland; and Europeans—as citizens and consumers—are ever more frequently affected by decisions taken in Brussels. Yet for only a minority of citizens does the EU seem like a genuine moral community, an entity that inspires attachment, "care," or even just meaningful political concern. In short, this supranational, unidentified entity lacks what some philosophers have described as an "identification mechanism for the civic body as a whole."[7]

It's against this background—the perceived lack of identification and attachment—that the concept of constitutional patriotism has been increasingly debated across Europe, even if its exact relevance has not always been fully spelled out by its proponents. In fact, in many ways, visions of a European constitutional patriotism might seem decidedly absurd. Edmund Burke put it bluntly: "men are not tied to one another by papers and seals. They are led to associate by resemblances, by conformities, by sympathies. It is with nations"—and, one might presume, with Europe—"as with individuals."

Yet even if papers and seals could tie men (and women) together—about which constitution are Europe's citizens supposed to be patriotic? The more than 80,000 pages of the European Union's rules and regulations, the *acquis communautaire*? A shorter written constitution—but still falling far short of the brevity of the American one—as has been attempted in the early years of the twenty-first century? Or should Europeans' hearts simply warm to the Euro-anthem, and should they pledge allegiance to the star-spangled blue banner and other symbols notorious for their artificiality? And if such ideas are rejected, would becoming post-national (or supuranational) not amount to becoming "post-emotional" (or perhaps supra-emotional)? Can affect not be made to work for democracy at all beyond the nation-state?

Then there's also the—somewhat more urgent, one might say, and certainly more real—question of what constitutes a "patriot act" in countries that feel threatened by outside enemies, or inside enemies, for that matter. Many in the United States have been searching for a conception of patriotism that might give significant leeway for dissent or even civil disobedience; but just repeating over and over that "dissent is patriotic" clearly isn't enough. Patriotism, it seems, would have to be linked with a larger moral vision for the country, perhaps even a global vision, if one does not hold to what might be called the "vacuum theory of patriotism": the idea that unless the forces of light engage in patriot talk, the topic will be captured by the forces of darkness. But perhaps that's false: perhaps *any* patriot talk furthers illiberal tendencies, rather than preempting them.

Finally—and briefly—constitutional patriotism has even been advocated as a form of belonging in deeply divided post-war societies: for example, the head of Bosnian Muslims has explicitly called for a pan-Bosnian constitutional patriotism—an odd idea, many might say, given that even the most optimistic observers of the Balkans would concede that the Bosnian constitution is a convoluted, "consociational" legal monster that freezes living, breathing human beings in their supposedly singular "ethnic identities" (or, if you like, "civil war identities").[8] If this seems overambitious, it's not unreasonable, though, to think that constitutional patriotism might be relevant in established democracies with increasingly diverse populations who seek to establish a kind of "civic

minimum" to determine how they want to live together—
and who, can belong, and who perhaps, shouldn't.

The idea of constitutional patriotism has been shadowed by many—and often seemingly contradictory—suspicions. On the one hand, constitutional patriotism—
again, understood as a post-national, universalist form of
democratic political allegiance—is rejected on account of
its abstract or, as an especially inappropriate metaphor
goes, "bloodless" quality. Given the universalist morality
at the heart of constitutional patriotism, so the critics
argue, there is no reason to identify with any particular
polity. In other words, constitutional patriotism is accused
of being a kind of aspirational oxymoron, in which the
universalist part, indicated by the concept of constitutionalism, will always drive out the idea of loyalty, indicated
by the concept of patriotism.

However, a second criticism holds almost exactly the
opposite from the first; here it's argued that constitutional
patriotism, while appearing universalist, is in fact particular through and through. According to what one might
call a "genealogical" critique, it is claimed that constitutional patriotism might have been appropriate in the context where it originated—namely West Germany, a "half-
nation" with a sense of deeply compromised nationality
on account of its Nazi past. But, so the argument goes,
other countries do not have a comparably difficult past,
and therefore are better served by forms of liberal nationalism—nationalism, that is, which is concrete, passionate,
alive, and yet kept in check by liberalism. A further argument holds that other countries either have no constitutions (or at least no written constitutions, as in the United
Kingdom and Israel), or that they simply do not venerate
the constitution as a focal point of democratic loyalty in

the way Germans might (or might not, in fact) do. In short, then, according to the genealogical critique, constitutional patriotism is a sort of particularism in universalist disguise—and one that might be foisted on Europe as a whole, if the advocates of a "European constitutional patriotism" have their way. In a strange fashion, Thomas Mann's nightmare—a German Europe, rather than a European Germany—might come true, after all.[9]

It's somewhat astonishing to note just how polarized debate has become around a supposedly anodyne concept. On the one hand, there are those who dismiss the idea as naively, if not recklessly, idealistic: a "pale thought born in the seminar room," as a former Justice of the German Constitutional Court once put it; one of Europe's most respected journalists, Joachim Fest, called it a typical "kind of professor's idea which is invented at the writing table, then further discussed by other professors," only to conclude: "a beautiful idea—but it doesn't work because people don't feel that way." In other words, "people" just want to be British, or Indian, or Irish-American, or Serb-Bosnian for that matter, not "constitutional patriots."

And yet many Americans, when, let's say, a professor of political theory laboriously expounds the supposedly professorial idea, react by saying, "Of course—it's what we do every day." And arguably the American "Creed" has always been the implicit reference point for advocates of constitutional patriotism; this was especially the case for European thinkers such as Jürgen Habermas, who first popularized the term in the late 1980s and who wanted the Germans (and other European countries) to move away from the notion of ethnically homogeneous nation-states. Another form of social cohesion is possible, philosophers like Habermas seemed to be saying, and you only

have to look across the Atlantic to see that it can work—
you only have to look to the land of what John H. Schaar
once termed "covenanted patriotism."

More recently, though, this situation appears almost to
have been reversed. The contrast between a non-ethnic,
constitutively open, and liberal universalist America, Jef-
ferson's "Empire of Liberty" and Emerson's "Asylum of
all Nations," on the one hand, and a nationalist Europe,
on the other, has been replaced by a quite different opposition: a post-national, postmodern, even post-heroic Europe, on one side, and a United States that appears to act
in all the normatively doubtful, aggressive ways that used
to be identified with ethnic nationalism. Suddenly it's dis-
covered that the American civic "Creed" might have been
associated all along with what Louis Hartz had called
"compulsive nationalism."[10]

It's a thought that might also engender second thoughts
about the concept of constitutional patriotism as such. Is
constitutional patriotism not always potentially illiberal,
authoritarian, or, as postmodernists might say, "normaliz-
ing"? Is civic allegiance not, when all is said and done,
the opposite of true individuality? Why spin theories that
justify or even reinforce what is, if we are to believe Mac-
Intyre, in any event a source of "moral danger"?

But, it seems, spin theories we must. What is rather
abstractly called "social integration" has become a problem, or, if one prefers less loaded language, a challenge,
in many different countries and across countries and for
different reasons, to be sure, and in different forms: "regional integration," as with the European Union, is not
the same as the "integration" of immigrants and minorities. There's a diffuse notion that globalization has reinforced the need for what is often referred to as a "sense

of belonging," a reconfiguration of collective identities, politically, legally, and, not least, emotionally. Sovereignty has become "frayed," as one scholar puts it, and citizenship "disaggregated."[11] Perhaps we might even say that what Todd Gitlin has observed about the United States—that it "invites anxiety about what it means to belong, because the national boundary is ideological, hence disputable and porous"—is now true for ever more countries.[12] Perhaps all the world is becoming America; less dramatically put (and also less threateningly, for some, no doubt), it has become harder to conceptualize both individual and collective "belonging" almost everywhere—the civic bond is in question.

And yet one can exaggerate this. Did people in the past feel more "at home in the world" somehow? Were the morals of membership unproblematic when, just to take the example of Europe, the twentieth century alone was characterized by recurring shifts in borders, and what sometimes has been referred to as the "three terrible e's": exterminations, expulsions, and exchanges (of populations, that is)? Surely, even with an increase in the overall number of civil wars, and with significant increases in migration, in many contexts membership has also become more secure.

All this is just to make the point that political theory must not turn into kitsch, by telling comforting (or disquieting) stories about the past. But it should provide the concepts, the languages, to allow citizens to rethink what they might or might not have in common, and what they perhaps should have in common. Nationalists have been doing this for centuries; cosmopolitans have now also begun telling different stories. I want to show that there is room—and a case—for a conception in between that incorporates the most attractive moral intuitions at the heart of liberal nationalism and cosmopolitanism. In particular, I want to claim that constitutional patriotism theorizes the civic bond in a way that is more plausible sociologically and that leads to more liberal political outcomes than its main "domestic" rival, liberal nationalism. Liberal nationalists have made much of the supposed "abstractness" of constitutional patriotism, but what liberal nationalists conceive as the core object of their theory—a singular "national culture"—is in fact *more* of an abstraction than a set of normative commitments centered on a constitution. And whereas liberal nationalism often relies tacitly on liberal legacies of tolerance in countries like Britain and Canada to render nationalism safe for liberal democracy—without, however, telling us how such legacies can be kept alive—constitutional patriotism offers us *concrete* normative resources—norms and values—for maintaining political regimes as well as for contesting them.

Why do such apparently minor academic differences matter? Because the languages we use for collective ethical self-clarification—"who do we want to be?"—do matter for actual policy outcomes: a liberal nationalism that essentially reifies "national culture" is likely to opt for immigration and integration policies that are highly assimilationist; it's also more likely to place limits on political dissent and insist, for instance, that heroic national histories can't be questioned since they allegedly need to serve as sources of "national pride."

An Overview

I'll start this essay with a brief conceptual history of constitutional patriotism. This is not just an exercise in antiquarianism, or a bit of scene setting; rather, it's a way of taking seriously what I've above already called the "genealogical" critique of constitutional patriotism. I shall argue that this genealogical critique is indeed not without force; while of course neither constitutionalism nor patriotism were invented by Germans, constitutional patriotism, as a theory distinct from both liberal nationalism and republican patriotism, was elaborated most clearly in post-war West Germany—and for clearly discernible historical reasons.

Moreover—and this has been less obvious even to the most informed students of constitutional patriotism—rather than being merely a universalist response to a nationalist past, constitutional patriotism has always relied on "supplements of particularity" to become effective as a form of political attachment.[13] In the German context constitutional patriotism has contained strong doses of what, by way of shorthand, I shall call "memory" and "militancy." Memory here refers primarily to a self-critical remembering of the Holocaust and the Nazi past; militancy, on the other hand, has been shown toward the enemies of democracy, mostly through judicial means such as banning political parties and restricting free speech. In other words, a militant democracy is explicitly *not* neutral about its own principles and values—and puts in place strong checks on those hostile (or perceived as hostile) to them.

Political agency, then, as envisaged by the proponents of constitutional patriotism, has been conceived as animated by a set of universalist norms, but enriched and strengthened by particular experiences and concerns. These particular experiences and concerns have been concentrated in what one might call two "negative contrasts," namely a contrast of present democracy with the evils of the past, and a contrast of present democracy with real or potential anti-democratic challenges.

I want to argue that memory and militancy were not accidental forms of particularity associated with constitutional patriotism; rather, there is an inherent normative connection to the universalist kernel of constitutional patriotism. Put in the vocabulary of "identity talk," memory and militancy (thus defined) reinforce "identity" through negative contrasts—with the past that is being repudiated, or with anti-democratic political actors in the present (or potentially in the future). Positive political principles do *imply* these negative contrasts, but this is not to say that all forms of constitutional patriotism would have to come with a strong emphasis on memory and militancy. In other words, and contrary to one of the most widespread clichés of our time, not every "identity" needs primarily to be "constructed" through an "Other." So the genealogical critique of constitutional patriotism, I claim, does not by itself invalidate the concept. There might be good reasons, however, not to put too much stress on memory and militancy as aspects of constitutional patriotism, as both have an illiberal side, and I shall say more about these pitfalls in the context of my discussion of the European Union.

I then move on to a more general theory of constitutional patriotism, which also seeks to elucidate as clearly as possible the *limits* of what a theory of constitutional patriotism can by itself prescribe. Constitutional patriotism, as explicated here, is a distinctive moral proposal, but it has only limited application. In particular, constitutional patriotism is not by itself a theory of justice: it is what has been called a *normatively dependent* concept, that is, it depends on a wider theory of justice to gain substantive normative content.[14] And what I offer here is a distinctly *moral* reading of constitutional patriotism by attaching it to a moral background theory centerd on the idea of *sharing political space on fair terms*. But it's perfectly plausible to offer different versions that make constitutional patriotism normatively dependent on different background theories of justice. What is not plausible, however, is to reduce constitutional patriotism to what might be called a "purely positivist" reading. Such positivism would hold that we have "constitutional patriotism" whenever we observe people being attached to persistent political arrangements, without any further normative specifications.

In previous discussions of the concept even the most fundamental question of what constitutional patriotism actually *is* has often remained unclear. Partly through an analogy with liberal nationalism—which in turn trades on analogies with the family and other special moral relationships—constitutional patriotism has been described very generally as an "attachment," or as an "identity," but also as a "resistance to identification."[15] Liberal nationalists have at least been clear on the idea that *national identity comes first*, so to speak, and a particular political morality based on "fellow-feeling" is then in more or less direct ways supposed to "follow" from such an identity.[16] Advocates of constitutional patriotism, on the other hand, have found it much harder to be clear on what comes first: an "attachment" to universal values, which is then realized in a particular political setting? Or do we start with a particular polity, which, as long as it meets certain standards of what we construe as liberal democratic universalism, could and should be made the object of a kind of civic loyalty?[17]

It's also often been unclear which particular overall purpose a theory of constitutional patriotism is supposed to serve. Is constitutional patriotism about stabilizing expectations of political behavior—in other words, is it ultimately an account of how to generate political *stability*? Put differently, is constitutional patriotism essentially a variety of political liberalism, which in the end is supposed to ensure the stability of societies divided by deep disagreements? Or is constitutional patriotism in fact a form of what might be termed *civic empowerment*? In other words, does it potentially translate the attachment to political principles into kinds of political action that can turn *against* governments, and even destabilize them—through civil disobedience, for example? As with the question of particular polities and values, those interested in a clarification of the concept might legitimately ask about priorities: does stability come first, or does empowerment? And if they go together, what is the condition of possibility of the two going together? These are the questions taken up in the more general chapter, where I'll suggest that constitutional patriotism is indeed what you might call Janus-faced: oriented both toward stability *and* civic empowerment.

In the last chapter I'll then examine an area in which, according to many political thinkers, constitutional patriotism appears to be particularly attractive or at least useful: the challenge of supranational "belonging," as exemplified here by the European Union. I don't want to say too much for now about the rather complex argument about European constitutional patriotism that I try to develop in the final chapter, but I want to stress that what I offer in the chapter are ways of thinking differently about these issues, not clear-cut policy prescriptions in the way that, in my view, academics are sometimes too eager to produce for Brussels. The reader—and citizen, I also hope—will have to decide where to take these thoughts, if they can be taken anywhere at all.

Finally, a very brief word on the usually much-dreaded subject of "method." Here, two clarifications are in order: first, almost always discussions of liberal nationalism, constitutional patriotism, and similar concepts appear to come down to decisions along the lines of "Well, I take a little more emotion," while someone else might say, "Well, I'll get by—just by reason." Put less frivolously, it might appear that these debates are ultimately undecidable, unless we actually had very complex *empirical* studies that would somehow yield the right moral-psychological "mixture" of reason and emotion in, for instance, motivating solidarity, or making citizens want to defend their liberal-democratic institutions. While political and legal theorists are sometimes too quick to discard empirical approaches—to put it mildly—it is in this case not unduly pessimistic to think that no such clear-cut results are likely to emerge anytime soon. Thus, one ought to be as clear as possible about which moral-psychological assumptions enter arguments about loyalty, attachment, and belonging, how plausible they could be in general, and also to what extent we can do without them.

Second, in debates about post-national or cosmopolitan forms of political attachment, especially in the case of the EU, there is also an unfortunate tendency for opponents to make facts into values—and for proponents, and Euro-cheerleaders in particular, to make values into facts. What follows is, I am afraid to say, indeed part fact and part value—but I shall at least try to delineate which is which.

One

A BRIEF HISTORY
OF CONSTITUTIONAL PATRIOTISM

> Every collective identity, also
> a postnational one, is much more
> concrete than the ensemble of moral,
> legal and political principles around
> which it crystallizes.
> —Jürgen Habermas

> "Man" is really "the German."
> —Marx, *The German Ideology*

NEITHER CONSTITUTIONALISM nor patriotism were invented by Germans. Yet, constitutional patriotism, as a theory distinct from liberal nationalism, traditional republican patriotism, and cosmopolitanism, was elaborated most clearly in post-war West Germany. This does not mean that it constituted a response to exclusively German problems, as critics have never tired of claiming. After all, various countries in Western Europe—even undivided ones—were facing challenges of "integration" and social cohesion. How was one to establish stable democracies and avoid repeating the political breakdowns of the interwar period? How was one to foster civic solidarity in countries segmented into different classes and different religious and ethnic groups? Who was to guard the new democratic constitutions—to take up Carl Schmitt's classic question?[1] And how would the antagonism with communism and the simultaneous demands for decolonization affect national self-understandings in the western part of the continent?

The Birth of Constitutional Patriotism Out of the Spirit of German Guilt: From Free Communication to Republican Loyalty

Perhaps some of the deepest roots of the idea of constitutional patriotism, as it later emerged in the thought of Jürgen Habermas, can be traced to the political interventions of the liberal philosopher Karl Jaspers in the immediate post-war period.[2] In his famous *The Question of German Guilt*, Jaspers drew seminal distinctions between criminal, moral, political, and metaphysical guilt. Definitions of criminal and moral guilt were relatively straightforward; political guilt, in Jaspers's conception, attached to all those living under cruel and unjust regimes; metaphysical guilt, finally, referred to a rupture in a deep level of solidarity that Jaspers assumed existed among all human beings.

In this context Jaspers also advocated a notion of "collective responsibility."[3] He opposed such a notion to the charge of "collective guilt" which he (and many others) felt was being levelled against Germany. At the same time, he linked collective responsibility with the question of German unity. According to Jaspers, a democratic political identity and proper social integration could only be achieved if the Germans shouldered collective responsibility. For Jaspers, even a negative past could become a source of social cohesion. In fact, he held that in the German case, not facing up to the past would make social cohesion difficult, if not impossible.

However, Jaspers's account of the institutional expression of the imperative to assume collective responsibility remained ambiguous. Had the Germans once and for all squandered their nation-state? If so, would this allow for the emergence of what Jaspers called the "true German as world citizen," or even, on a less hopeful cosmopolitan note, make the Germans take the place of the Jews as a "pariah"-nation? Or was the German nation to be a "pariah" for a certain time only, potentially regaining its statehood, or gaining a new form of post-nationalist statehood, after a period of political and moral "purification"?[4] The first option was suggested by Jaspers's remark in a letter to Hannah Arendt that "Germany is the first nation that, as a nation, has gone to ruin," but also by his admission that "now that Germany is destroyed, I feel at ease for the first time."[5]

In fact, Jaspers linked the idea of "working through the past" explicitly with a new kind of cosmopolitanism: the project of continuously contested memory and the idea of "universal membership" were to become inseparable— even if it remained unclear what precisely "universal membership" was supposed to entail. Jaspers repudiated his previous nationalism, which he had adopted from his teacher Max Weber, explicitly denying that a liberal political identity and a nation-state framework could go together for the Germans. He also insisted that, as much as moral guilt was a question for one's individual conscience, the only way to deal with German guilt as a whole was through "free public communication" and what he called the "solidarity of charitable struggle," instead of mutual moral condemnations.[6] This claim, rooted, in Jaspers's philosophy of free communication between equals, was eventually taken up by intellectuals who sought to establish an even tighter link between remembrance and a democratic political culture—by Jaspers's pupil Dolf Sternberger and, much later, and more importantly, by Jürgen Habermas.[7]

It would not be unfair to say that ultimately Jaspers was an apolitical thinker. He could not find any lasting institutional expression (or an affective one) for the connection between collective responsibility and democratic citizenship that he was advocating. However, he was not the only theorist in the aftermath of the War who was concerned with the question of whether political stability could be ensured through a particular civic identity, or, if you like, moral collective identity—as opposed to stability always having to be ensured by strong governments, if not authoritarian ones. After all, political and legal thinkers in post-war West Germany were haunted by the failure of the Weimar Republic. Germany's first republic had been based on what many saw as the world's most progressive constitution at the time, but Weimar had also been a "democracy without democrats," and, in the eyes of many observers, it had partly been rendered vulnerable by the most democratic clauses of the constitution—clauses and mechanisms which had eventually been abused by the enemies of democracy. Consequently, post-war thinkers were anxious whether a properly liberal democratic constitution could survive in a country (or half-country) like West Germany at all, other than through the backing of the Allies.

Not surprisingly, then, Carl Schmitt's question—who guards the constitution against the enemies of democracy?—came to be central to many post-war legal debates. Candidates for such guardianship ranged from a strong president (who would have been Schmitt's own choice) to the state bureaucracy, and even the trade unions. Soon, however, the Constitutional Court emerged as the main contender for the role of defending democracy against its enemies. The crucial step in this direction was the so-called Lüth decision of 1958, in which the Court held that the "objective principles" embodied in the Basic Rights permeated the entire legal order. With this decision, the Court bootstrapped itself into a position where judicial review of almost any legal and political decision became legitimate.

But the Court also began to occupy itself with the question of how citizens could be made "to-feel-at-home-in-the-state," or, as the wonderful German phrase goes, *"Sich-in-disem-Staat-zu-Hause-Fühlen."* The main jurisprudential approach that seemed available for addressing this concern about potential "civic homelessness" was the "integration theory" initially proposed by Rudolf Smend.[8] Smend had been one of the most important opponents of legal positivism during the Weimar Republic; he had argued that lawyers should draw on a mixture of legal theory and sociology to understand political integration as a truly dynamic process. In this context Smend distinguished personal, functional, and objective factors of integration. The first related to personalities, whether that of a monarch or a strong parliamentary leader; the second involved institutions like parliament; the third, finally, referred to basic laws and liberties, understood not so much as defensively directed against the state than as embodying shared political values or principles. Smend further held that "democratic integration might best be accomplished through plebiscites, and, in particular, what he called "democratic symbols." Such symbols could include the flag and the national anthem, but also a state's territory. Crucial, however, was a general trust and pride in the political system.

It's worth remembering that during the 1920s Smend had entertained an ambivalent relationship with liberal democracy, to say the least: he had come to think that Mussolini's fascism might be a more effective way of achieving democratic integration. After the War, however, he turned out to be one of the most important legal theorists to support the new democratic constitution. He and his many followers now argued for a more sociological and cultural focus on the polity. For them, the Constitution was indeed squarely at the center of the political order; but even more importantly in light of the question of "integration," the Constitution embodied an order of values which derived from the political culture and traditions of a particular country. Decisions by the Constitutional Court were to be based on these values, which, at least according to Smend, could be put in a clear hierarchy. In turn the deliberations and decisions of the Constitutional Court itself would contribute to social integration; rather than being alienated through "government by judges," citizens would come to understand their political system better and identify with its institutions.

Thus in legal theory, and also in actual fact, the Constitution assumed an extraordinary position in post-war German thinking about politics. While the Weimar constitution had been seen as a great intellectual and political achievement initially, and then de facto failed disastrously, it was more or less the other way around after 1945: legal theorists regarded the Constitution as a problematic construct at the beginning—a list of articles seemingly imposed from outside, deliberated over with hardly any publicity, and unable to withstand serious threats to democracy. Yet, as time went on, the Constitution proved not only its resilience; it also proved its enormous *relevance* in ordering political life.[9] In fact, the Constitutional Court eventually developed into the most respected public institution of the country, alongside the central bank.

It was against this background that the political scientist Dolf Sternberger explicitly introduced his concept of constitutional patriotism on the occasion of the thirtieth birthday of the Federal Republic.[10] Sternberger had been a close associate of Jaspers and became the doyen of democratic political theory in West Germany after the War. As early as 1959, Sternberger had thought about a "patriotic sentiment in the constitutional state"; and in the early 1960s he had developed the notion of *Staatsfreundschaft* [friendship with, or, rather, toward, the state]; in 1970 the word *Verfassungspatriotismus* itself made its first appearance.[11] Sternberger framed this rather awkwardly named "state friendship" as what he called a "passionate rationality": a kind of civic reason that would make citizens identify with the democratic state and, not least, defend it against its enemies.[12]

To give his conception of constitutional patriotism theoretical coherence, Sternberger drew on Aristotle's and Hannah Arendt's republicanism; to lend it historical credibility, he excavated a tradition of patriotism stretching back to Aristotle which, he claimed, had not been linked to the nation. Sternberger argued that at least until the end of the eighteenth century, all forms of patriotism had been constitutional patriotism—understood as the love of the laws and common liberties. In other words, constitutional patriotism was to be understood as a return to pre-national patriotism.

However, as much as Sternberger was trying to transcend conventional notions of the nation-state, it would be hard to deny that he remained substantially indebted to familiar traditions of German *étatisme*. Sternberger, who was born in 1907, had been profoundly scarred by the experience of Weimar's failure. It was not surprising, then, that he focused primarily on loyalty to the state and, somewhat more narrowly, to the rule of law, rather than on specific civil liberties or the social rights which a constitution might also guarantee. Constitutional patriotism was distinctly *not* meant as a form of civic empowerment; it was still much more a form of what German political theorists in an almost untranslatable phrase call *Staatsbewußtsein*—a "consciousness of belonging to the state."

Perhaps not so surprisingly, then, Sternberger also explicitly called upon the "friends of the Constitution" to defend the polity. He thereby linked constitutional patriotism to the concept of a *wehrhafte* or *streitbare Demokratie*—that is, a "militant democracy" capable of defending itself against its internal and external enemies.[13] For instance, when the writer Heinrich Böll suggested "mercy" for Ulrike Meinhof of the "Baader-Meinhof gang" in 1972, Sternberger shot back that "the democratic state is also a state . . . render unto the state what is the state's, Böll!"[14] Sternberger's "friends of the Constitution" were thereby polemically opposed to the "enemies of the Constitution"—a highly contested concept used mostly in the 1970s for terrorists and those suspected of supporting them. This idea of "constitutional enmity" justified the restriction of civil liberties, the choice of jobs in the civil service in particular, and, to this day, has left a legacy of illiberal legislation designed to deal with those suspected of opposing the Constitution.

Constitutional patriotism, then, became closely associated with "militant democracy," a concept that in turn had first been defined by the German exile political scientist Karl Loewenstein in 1938.[15] At that time, one European country after the other had been taken over by authoritarian movements using democratic means to disable democracy. Loewenstein argued that democracies were incapable of defending themselves against fascist movements if they continued to subscribe to "democratic fundamentalism," "legalistic blindness," and an "exaggerated formalism of the rule of law."[16] Part of the new challenge was that, according to Loewenstein, fascism had no proper intellectual content, relying on a kind of "emotionalism" with which democracies could not compete. Consequently, democracies had to find political and legislative answers to anti-democratic forces—such as banning parties and militias. They should also restrict the rights to assembly and free speech, and, not least, the activities of those suspected of supporting fascist movements—who could be "guilty by association."[17] As Loewenstein put it, "fire should be fought with fire"; and that fire, in his view, could only be lit by a new, "disciplined," or even "authoritarian" democracy.[18]

This idea of militant democracy subsequently became highly influential in the Federal Republic. It was used to justify the banning of the Nazi Socialist Reich Party and the Communist Party by the Constitutional Court in the 1950s, and, later, the draconian measures against those guilty of (suspected) association with terrorists.[19] The Court's decisions and the rhetoric used by successive West German governments made it clear that democracy was to be as militant about the Left as the Right; in other words, militancy was framed as a form of "anti-totalitarianism," directed as much against the communist threat from the East as against any revivals of the brown menace from the past. The legal basis for bans and for restricting rights—for anti-democratic measures supposed to serve democracy—was the so-called free democratic basic order. The Court had coined the phrase and elaborated it in its judgments in the 1950s; this "order" consisted of the very values which, according to the Court, were permeating the entire legal system. Thus emerged what has been called "democratic anti-extremism," a defensive stance that, by definition, assumed the symmetry of threats from the Right and the Left.[20] Critics, however, charged from the beginning that this anti-extremism could easily be instrumentalized against legitimate opposition (especially left-wing opposition), while, at the same time, it did little to help deal with the Nazi past. If anything, its implicit equation of Soviet Communism (and its alleged foreign agents) and Nazism seemed to relativize the specific evil of Nazism.

Against the background of such peculiar legal traditions, it should become clear that the primary purpose of what one might call Sternberger's "protective constitutional patriotism" was to ensure political stability; this in turn contributed to what Sternberger construed as the ultimate purpose (or concept) of politics—the establishment of peace. *Protective patriotism* of this sort entailed a low level of political tolerance, but also strong pedagogical elements. Its moral substance was a conception of civic Aristotelian friendship, through which citizens would make claims on each other, but through which the state could also make claims on its citizens.

The affective ties of Sternberger's constitutional patriotism, you might say, were mainly vertical, rather than horizontal—citizens would "care for" concrete, particular institutions by identifying their interests in peace and protected liberty with those of the institutions.[21] Their attachment was "political" in the sense that they expressed a continuous will to uphold such particular political institutions—and feelings motivating this will were, above all, pride in having built these institutions and in possessing them now. In this vision, then, patriotism was not a matter of uncomplicated belonging or a kind of "feeling at home" that could be taken for granted; instead, it was based on a political *achievement* and, no less important, on an *adversarial* relationship with democracy's enemies, real or presumed.[22] In the end, loyalty was owed to political and legal institutions as embodiments of a particular constitutional tradition.[23]

Sternberger's constitutional patriotism, it should be emphasized, did not exclude national solidarity with the citizens of East Germany, who, legally, remained citizens of the Federal Republic and thus, in theory, subject to its Constitution. In that sense, constitutional patriotism was from the start "de-territorialized": it was open to others as yet outside the specific territory of constitutional patriots who might wish to join in patriotic sentiment. But it also retained particularity; in fact, some might say, too much particularity. After all, only East Germans were hypothetically in a position to join the community of constitutional patriots, and Sternberger's conception of constitutional patriotism certainly did not put into question West Germany's then highly ethnic definition of citizenship. Advocates of Sternberger's constitutional patriotism tacitly relied on a historical, or even ethnic, framework for constitutional patriotism.[24]

Habermas's Constitutional Patriotism: Toward "Rational Collective Identities"

Jürgen Habermas first advanced his version of constitutional patriotism during the so-called "historians' dispute" of 1986.[25] On a purely historiographical level, this acrimonious controversy revolved around the singularity of National Socialism and the Holocaust and, in particular, their comparability to Stalinism and the Gulag. On a political level, however, both the participants in the dispute and many observers felt that what was really at stake was German "collective identity." In particular, Habermas claimed that a number of conservative historians were attempting to "normalize" German identity, and facilitating the return of a conventional form of national pride. This new national consciousness, in Habermas's view, was to shore up the stability of the political system and, indirectly, that of the Western Alliance as a whole. Against such a form of uncomplicated national pride, Habermas advocated constitutional patriotism as the only permissible form of political identification for West Germans.

In accordance with Sternberger, Habermas portrayed constitutional patriotism as a conscious affirmation of *political* principles. However, he did not think that an unproblematic return to a pre-national (and premodern) patriotism centered on civic friendship was possible: the conclusion that emerged from Habermas's broader social theory—a theory which, especially in the rather simplified version presented here, might give the impression of being naively teleological, or overly "rationalist," or just an instance of a kind of Kohlbergian triumphalism of the pristine universal over "beclouded partiality," suspicions to which I'll return explicitly later on.[26]

Here's a simple, but, I hope, not caricatured version of the theory: the disenchantment of the modern world and its complex division into different spheres of value (such as the political, the economy, or the aesthetic) would render a straightforward return to an Aristotelian polity impossible. Individual and collective identities are no longer formed—or should no longer be formed—by uncritically internalizing religious or, for that matter, nationalist imperatives; put differently, an unproblematic reference to quasi-sacred objects, including the *patria*, is said to be no longer available. Instead, in a properly disenchanted world, individuals develop what Habermas, following the psychological models of Lawrence Kohlberg, has called "post-conventional identities": they learn to adopt as impartial a point of view as possible and to step back from their own desires and from the conventional social expectations with which society and its more particular institutions confront them. Identity becomes "de-centered," as individuals relativize what they want and what others expect from them in the light of wider moral considerations.

A similar story to what happens with individuals is said to unfold at the level of society.[27] The exercise of coercion over citizens can no longer be justified by reference to sacred or quasi-sacred sources; one way or another, directly or more indirectly, popular sovereignty becomes the sole source of legitimacy. Religious legitimacy is—or ought to be—abandoned alongside traditionalism and other apparently transcendent sources of authority. Democracy, in turn, needs rights and liberties, which by their very nature contain a universalist kernel. Their realization, however, requires a particular polity; de facto, they require the nation-state, the only political framework in which large-scale democracy has appeared in the modern world. Yet their universalist normative content always exceeds any necessarily particular realization in time.

Thus emerges what Habermas has termed "post-traditional society." This concept, one should hasten to add, does not imply that particularity has to be relentlessly purged, or that religion, tradition, "family values," and other forms of "conventional morality" are simply superseded; instead, they are, at least partially, reinterpreted in the light of the universalist claims and perspectives that also find expression—however imperfectly—as basic civil rights and as constitutional norms more generally. In other words, citizens are asked to reflect critically upon particular traditions and group identities in the name of shared universal principles. This also means that they have reflectively to endorse—or, for that matter, reject—the particular national traditions with which they find themselves confronted. Put differently, the cold light of reason is not supposed to be a permanent glare, in which the dimly and warmly perceived objects of tradition appear as naked and insufficient, but rather a searchlight that is employed from time to time to examine and, if necessary, clean up the complex store of ideas, styles, and normative frameworks that shape our lives not very consciously, for the most part. But we never replace everything at the same time, which is why the "horror vision" of an entirely unattached, or, as the jargon of political philosophy has it, the "unencumbered self," does not apply here.[28] If we want to stick with the homey metaphors that communitarians often favor, it's a matter of good housekeeping, not philosophically prescribed homelessness.

So in this (of course, highly stylized) account, unconditional, or even unreflective, identification is then supposed to be replaced by dynamic and complex processes of identity-formation—that is, by open-ended political and legal learning processes. There is, according to this vision, no unchanging "object of identification," whether the nation or even, let's say, a historically specific constitution. What matters is a kind of critical, highly self-conscious back-and-forth between actually existing traditions and institutions, on the one hand, and the best universal norms and ideas that can be worked out, on the other. And the precise object is less important than the appropriately "post-conventional" stance that subjects attachments and loyalties to critical reflection and, if necessary, revision— and then further revision.

What unfolds at the level of the individual through social interaction needs a delicate web of communicative processes at the collective level: it is in a public sphere as porous as possible that collective identities are renegotiated. Such open-ended communication is a crucial precondition for what Habermas has termed the "rationalization of collective identities"—no doubt a term ideally chosen to confirm conservatives' worst suspicions about what already might appear as an excessively rationalist, or progressivist, style of theorizing. But it's as good as any, one might say, to capture the critical distancing from unquestioned inherited beliefs. What this vision—subtracting for a moment the quasi-technocratic-sounding language of "rationalization"—ultimately entails would be something like this: a sense of critical attachment, one might say, is formed both to the character of the society that emerges from collective learning processes, and to the very procedures and concretely situated practices which make such processes possible in the first place.

The privileged site for the formation of this kind of "rationalised identity"—and the emergence of proper constitutional patriotism—is thus the *public sphere*. And the purpose of such patriotism, you might say, is the normative *purification* of public argument, as opposed to the *protection* of the polity, which, as we have seen, had been the main purpose of Sternberger's version of constitutional patriotism—a vigilant, highly defensive, and, you might say, somewhat nervous form of patriotism. The primary question here is about the democratic quality of political culture, not the defense of a democracy perpetually under threat from potential anti-democrats or those prone to neglecting the public good.

According to Habermas, post-conventional, "reflexive" identities were most likely to emerge where national traditions had been put decisively into question and where citizens felt acutely ambivalent about affirming historical continuities. A prime example was of course the Federal Republic, which, at least according to Habermas, had developed a form of patriotism focused not so much on historical identities as on rights and democratic procedures. In short, West Germans were able to develop a more abstract patriotism, which pointed beyond itself to even more abstract and inclusive forms of political belonging.

Habermas thus added a much stronger universalist element to the original conception of constitutional patriotism. Yet he also sought to eliminate the statist and some of the republican elements in Sternberger's theory. The traditionally German idea of the state as a substantial, or even metaphysical, entity above and beyond society was to be replaced by the *Rechtsstaat*, the constitutional, rule-of-law–based state, on the one hand, and the *Sozialstaat*, or welfare state, on the other. The former was to give force to universal norms and guarantee democratic procedures, whereas the latter was to provide a material foundation for citizens' effective political participation. Most importantly, where Sternberger's patriotism had centered on democratic institutions worth defending, Habermas focused on the public sphere as providing a space for public reasoning among citizens. In the public sphere, citizens could recognize each other as free and equal, engage in democratic learning processes and subject each other's claims to the very universal principles which they endorsed patriotically.

Territory, organization, and the monopoly of legitimate violence (including the violence against constitutional enemies), the traditional reference points for the state, were displaced by an emphasis on an open-ended process of communication. Such a process was formally underpinned by the rights guaranteed through the constitution and materially by the security provided through the welfare state. Citizenship consisted of effective access to this communication process among free and equal citizens, rather than passive, inherited nationality. Where Sternberger's civic friendship had essentially focused on the state, Habermas envisaged civic solidarity as an outcome of unconstrained discourse leading to mutual civic recognition, and an ongoing process of mutual learning.

As Ciaran Cronin has pointed out, in the early versions of this argument, "communicative processes" were still located outside actual political institutions.[29] A society's self-understanding was to be shaped by debates among politicians, intellectuals, journalists, and academic specialists. A prime example for such a debate was the *Historikerstreit* itself. While obviously revolving around historiographical questions, the ultimate issues were "who do we want to be?" and "how do we want to position ourselves to our past in light of this identity?" Identity, in short, had to be based on public interpretations in the light of norms, rather than on ascriptive, "pre-political" criteria. However, this was not simply a matter of replacing national with "post-national" identity. "Identity" itself had to become de-centered and even, to some extent, ambivalent. At the same time, the process of identity-formation itself had to be rendered more open, dynamic, and fluid.

Sources, Supplements, and Solidarity

Already at the time of Habermas's initial formulation of his conception of constitutional patriotism, criticisms were levelled that were to reappear in the arguments of Anglo-American liberal nationalists many years later. In particular, numerous critics doubted whether this conception could yield attachment to a *particular* polity. In other words, given the central place of universalist norms in Habermas's theory, the question was posed whether constitutional patriotism could ground a *distinctive* identity. After all, "something prior to constitutional principles determines who falls under their authority."[30] Alternatively, why should those supporting universalist moral norms not give their loyalty to polities which realize them in a fuller sense or a more coherent fashion? Constitutional patriotism, at first sight at least, seems to beg this very question.

Habermas himself presented one answer to this problem. He stressed that the particular—in fact unique—experience of National Socialism had to be the implicit reference point for German constitutional patriotism. Only after the ultimate evil of Nazism had Germany, at least its Western part, finally and fully embraced the Enlightenment and firmly anchored itself in the West. He affirmed that "our patriotism cannot hide the fact that in Germany democracy has taken root in the motives and the hearts of citizens, at least of the younger generation, after Auschwitz—and in a way only through the shock of this moral catastrophe."[31] And he added that "the overcoming of fascism forms the particular historical perspective from which a post-national identity centered on the universalist principles of the rule of law and democracy understands itself."[32] After all, "conventional morality," in the sense of obeying law and order, following "common sense," or acting according to national traditions had all spectacularly failed in preventing the moral catastrophe of the Third Reich.

There was, then, a certain *dialectic* to the fascist experience. It had been *aufgehoben*, that is, both transcended and negatively preserved, in a new post-fascist identity. Such an identity could be based only on traditions which had been reflected upon and passed the critical "filter" of Auschwitz. As Habermas put it: "Tradition means, after all, that we continue something as unproblematic, which others have started and demonstrated. We normally imagine that these 'predecessors,' if they stood before us face to face, could not completely deceive us, that they could not play the role of a deus malignus. I for one think that this basis of trust has been destroyed by the gas chambers."[33] Consequently, post-fascist identity *in particular* had to be post-traditional, or better, post-traditionalist.

So as with Jaspers, remembrance was linked to free public communication and, in particular, the public contestation of the past. Rather than enshrining a particular view of the past with sacralized rituals, interpretations of the past had to be renegotiated in an open public sphere. The controversies surrounding, for instance, trials, the extension of statutes of limitations, films, and monuments could all contribute to a process of moral self-clarification, as long as claims about memories were subjected to shared public reason.[34] This was true even if such shared public reason could itself not be isolated from controversy and disagreement. Here the hope was that controversial reflections on standards for treating the past would themselves contribute to finding a core political morality.

Memory would thus unfold a motivational power and supplement the universalist norms at the heart of constitutional patriotism. It would furnish the basis for a democratic consciousness.[35] This consciousness was not so much a matter of achievement, as with Sternberger's pride in the post-fascist democratic institutions of the Federal Republic (although Habermas also occasionally stressed these democratic institutions); even less was it a matter of unproblematic belonging. Identity was not to be understood in static (or, for that matter, statist) terms—it was constituted precisely by a continuous civic self-interrogation and open argument about the past, and, not least, the purging of problematic continuities with that past. In short, it was understood as a *process*.

Potentially, this process also had a more elaborate theoretical justification, as dealing with the past could be said to have an inherent connection with democracy. Memories, rather than being monolithic and serving as the instruments of nationalism, would always be conflicted, contested, and competing in an open public sphere. But, after all, democracy itself is a form of contained conflict. Rather than aiming for some elusive "thick" social consensus in which one narrative of the past is enthroned, arguing about the past within liberal legality and on the basis of what has been called an "economy of moral disagreement" could itself be a means of fostering social cohesion and solidarity. This would be precisely the solidarity of "charitable struggle" Jaspers had already talked about in the late 1940s.[36]

More importantly perhaps, one might say that democracy itself is about reiterated moments of collective responsibility, in which the governed examine the record of the governors (and their promises for the future, needless to say). By definition, democracies committed to the notion of accountability cannot forget at least their immediate past, whereas under less accountable forms of government the past is often mythologized, or perhaps even eradicated. Accountability in turn presumes some kind of autonomy—after all, politicians will not be held accountable for what is beyond their control. In turn, assuming responsibility for the past—or even guilt—would strengthen, rather than damage, autonomy. In that sense, one could at the least speak of a loose conceptual connection between autonomy, accountability, and memory, even though of course the sheer complexity of day-to-day political life would make this a very loose connection indeed.

But, then again, a note of scepticism is also in order, as there are good arguments for weakening the very connection I've just claimed exists: after all, it is ultimately the judicial branch that has to deal with the past, rather than the legislature or government. It's not unreasonable to think that democracy is primarily about the assertion of *collective* agency over the future, not a reckoning with the past. And, for the most part, the judiciary is only in a position to deal with *individual* cases that occurred in the past. Legislatures and governments can officially acknowledge the past, and of course pass laws dealing with restitution and reparation. But as far as the inner logic of institutions is concerned—their "spirit," to paraphrase Montesquieu—the past appears to be a matter for the courts. Constitutional liberalism—and not democracy as the ideal of a collective trying to master its own fate over time—is thus the answer to a past of mass atrocity. But if that is correct, then concentrating on memory might encourage both a juridification of politics and a potentially very limiting focus on isolated individuals, rather than democratic collectives and their actions. I'll have more to say on this in the European context in the third and final chapter.

Let me just claim for now that "coming to terms with the past" was a shared, and necessarily particular, activity for post-war Germans. But this also meant that in Germany there was no prima facie question about the particular context of constitutional patriotism. Patriotism would call for the repudiation of a particular past in the name of universal moral values. It would also call for the institution of political procedures to deal with moral arguments about the accountability of particular perpetrators and the claims of particular victims. Universal values were instantiated in a specific context shaped by a particular past and the common experience of trying to realize universal values in an effort to overcome that past.

Present-day Germans had to assume collective responsibility for the past, as "a kind of intersubjective liability" or debt arising from the "historical complex of forms of life that have been passed on from generation to generation," as Habermas put it.[37] It was not "collective guilt" that was passed on, but rather the cultural contexts and "forms of life" that might have facilitated crimes in the past. German law in fact does recognize cultural influence as a factor mitigating guilt. But neither Habermas nor German law see this as a kind of "collective guilt" attaching directly to the descendants of the perpetrators.[38] As Habermas put it,

> our own life is linked to the life context in which Auschwitz was possible not by contingent circumstances but intrinsically. Our form of life is connected with that of our parents and grandparents through a web of familial, local, political, and intellectual traditions that is difficult to disentangle— that is, through a historical milieu that made us what and who we are today. None of us can escape this milieu, because our identities, both as individuals and as Germans, are indissolubly interwoven with it.[39]

This intersubjective and intergenerational liability provided an additional answer to the criticism that "the liberal state has no home, and generates no loyalty toward generations, which, being either dead or unborn, form no part of the contract."[40] Generations did not form part of a "contract"—yet the suffering of the victims imposed a debt of "intersubjective liability" on successive generations—binding them together, though of course often also sometimes alienating them from one another . . .

Some Consequences and Peculiarities of "German" Constitutional Patriotism

The purpose of Habermas's constitutional patriotism was not so much protection as "purification" of the public sphere and political culture more widely, as well as the promotion of universalist moral principles. It was in no sense culturally neutral, since patriotism also required a particular, highly critical attitude toward national culture. On an affective level, it did not so much draw on a feeling of pride, and it did not simply "redirect" existing emotions from one object, the pre-political nation, to the political constitution.[41] Rather, it brought into play a much more complex set of emotions; this set contained guilt, shame, and, possibly, pride, as far as the democratic achievements of the post-war period were concerned.[42] Arguably it also included anger and indignation—with respect to the past, but also with regard to failures to live up to constitutional norms in the present. Constitutional patriotism, in this original formulation, produced solidarity rather indirectly through the common contestation of the past, as well as the common goal of promoting universal norms, yet perhaps its most morally significant form of solidarity (and caring) was reserved for the victims, rather than present fellow citizens.[43]

It's important to point out that constitutional patriotism, in its initial formulations, was never intended as an especially inclusive form of membership. There was an almost automatic assumption that these specific demands were directed at German citizens—the "we" of constitutional patriots appeared not to be in question.[44] At least initially, then, constitutional patriotism as a form of political attachment was decidedly not a solution to any kind of multicultural predicament or any "challenge of integration," and it was in fact ironic that it was elaborated and flourished in a polity with a strictly ethnic definition of citizenship and an extreme version of "ethnic-priority immigration."[45]

When the emphasis on militancy (as in Sternberger's account) and the stress on memory (as in Habermas's theory), merged, the result could be measures like the 1985 law against the "Auschwitz lie." Based on the theory of criminal libel, this particular law made denial of the Holocaust into an insult punishable by up to one year in prison.[46] The relevant insult here was not just seen as being directed against the immediate victims (and possibly their descendants)—it was also an offense to the self-understanding of the German polity as having repudiated a certain vision of the German past. As many advocates of free speech pointed out, the supposedly liberal loyalty of constitutional patriotism seemed to have produced a decidedly illiberal result. Yet, the defenders of the law would have argued that for any democratic deliberation, or, to use Jaspers's term, "free communication," about the past to take place at all, some of what Michael Ignatieff has called "impermissible lies" had to be eliminated.[47] Claiming that the Holocaust was a product of the Zionist imagination was a way not just of denying the dignity of the victims, but also of denying the dignity of one's democratic interlocutors. In the absence of agreement on basic historical facts, not even a proper "economy of moral disagreement" about what the past meant could be constructed.[48] Consequently, denial would make it simply impossible for any legitimacy to emerge from democratic contestation.

The law, then, was to fulfill a triple function: it was publicly to preserve historical truth, actively ensure a form of democratic exclusion and facilitate social integration among democrats committed to working through a difficult past. Yet it remained an open question whether it had to be the task of the *government* to concern itself with the beliefs its citizens held about historical events, even if one conceded that these beliefs were held for reasons and that sometimes these reasons should be seen as morally unacceptable. This still left the question whether the "elimination of impermissible lies" should not be left to civil society in an open process of contestation. This process might have included the shaming or marginalization of those clinging to denial. Instead the juridification of "working through the past" remained a distinctive feature of German political culture, even though making arguments about the past into a matter of legality could appear to be in direct conflict with the civic ideal of "charitable struggle."

A Professors's Dream . . . ?

This brief retelling of the emergence of a distinctive vision of constitutional patriotism has highlighted the historical circumstances and conceptual contexts in which the idea of constitutional patriotism was conceived. In itself, it is of course no surprise that constitutional patriotism has particular origins—how could it not? After all, "the universal has no voice, no authentic representative of its own"; the universal "can only appear through something particular; only a particular can make the universal known."[49]

More interesting is the fact that constitutional patriotism has relied on, so to speak, particular "supplements of particularity"—or, put differently, a constellation of subsidiary concepts which have allowed the universalist morality at the center of constitutional patriotism to be embedded within a (necessarily) particular political culture. Sternberger's "protective patriotism" became linked with the idea of militant democracy, whereas Habermas's "purifying patriotism"—oriented toward the public sphere, rather than the state—understood itself as relying on particular public memories, and on the contestation of public memories.

However, while the association of constitutional patriotism with militancy and memory, respectively, was due to the peculiar situation of post-war West Germany, there are, I wish to suggest, also important conceptual links between the morality of constitutional patriotism, militancy, and memory. Clearly, these three abstractions are located in different conceptual spaces, so to speak, but the imperatives of purification and protection are nevertheless in a meaningful way connected to the very idea of constitutional patriotism: those who subscribe to universalist liberal democratic values will see their past in a different light, and they will want to draw a legal and political line so far as the possibility of endangering these values is concerned. Clearly, to what extent actual citizens feel different about their pasts and to what extent democratic militancy is elaborated before any particular threat emerges are open empirical questions and will depend on much that is contingent. Existing national traditions will one way or another have a profound influence on the shape and style of a constitutional patriotism.

Constitutional patriotism is, then, as Ciaran Cronin has pointed out, not so much post-national as it is post-*nationalist*. Nationality is not somehow "suppressed" or purged, although it is, to use a somewhat ugly phrase, "de-centered." It was Benedict Anderson who once pointed out that "if one wished to see modern world history as an endless soap opera, in every country, the one character centrally cast in each interminable episode would be one's own nation." Constitutional patriotism does not make the nation-character die; it merely relegates him (or her) to a supporting role.

A constitutional patriotism with a richer account of memory and militancy does not simply turn into a particularly liberal variant of liberal nationalism. Superficially, there are, of course, similarities: liberal nationalists might also ask co-nationals to adopt a critical attitude toward a problematical past; in fact, it is hard to see how they would *not* counsel an attitude which is, at least to some extent, similar to what Habermas advocated for the Germans after 1945. They will also call upon co-nationals to defend a "liberal way of life," if necessary, although they might perhaps even turn out to be more tolerant than some constitutional patriots.

Yet an essential moral difference remains: in the eyes of real liberal nationalists, nationality carries an unquestioned (and, it seems, unquestionable) ethical significance. It is, after all, what people (allegedly) *feel* themselves to be. Constitutional patriotism, on the other hand, concedes only a pragmatic (and, in all likelihood, temporary) significance to nationality. It agrees with liberal na-

tionalism that particularity—in the form of particular political communities in which some human beings are
privileged over others—is not per se illegitimate. It also
agrees with liberal nationalism that such communities are
the only way to attain certain "relationship goods." But
nationality, for constitutional patriotism, does not generate these goods; and, in particular, it is not an extension
of (and does not constitute an analogy with) the family.

Thus constitutional patriotism is not an example of the
kind of pristine and politically impractical universalism
that some caricatures have made it out to be, but neither
is it reducible to its genesis in a particular nation with a
uniquely problematic past, as critics have claimed—critics, that is, who've essentially taken the view, "if I can't
get you on the universalism charge, I'll get you on particularism." But "empty universalism" is not enough of an
objection by liberal nationalists; and genealogy cannot
automatically count as critique.

Now, this defense doesn't yet in any way answer the
question whether constitutional patriotism really is of
wider relevance—this is the question I want to engage in
the next chapter. Before leaving the conceptual history of
constitutional patriotism behind, however, I just want to
stress that throughout its brief life in West Germany itself, constitutional patriotism always had very notable de-
tractors. Most importantly, critics argued that a need for
a proper national identity could not be satisfied by constitutional patriotism. Historians Hagen Schulze and Hans-
Peter Schwarz, for instance, argued that the national and
emotional "abstinence" of the purely "academic" *Verfassungspatriotismus* would leave the national question to
more sinister political forces, thus offering yet another
version of what I have called the "vacuum theory" of pa-

triotism. Moreover, the focus on the Constitution—as opposed to the state—frequently came under attack; constitutions, so the argument went, could not exist without a state, and they certainly could not be sovereign, as some supporters of constitutional patriotism allegedly claimed; and again and again *étatist* thinkers charged that the universalist values of the Constitution were insufficient to sustain social cohesion.[50] The writer Martin Walser went so far as to attack the concept as "embroidered blankets of solace over the gap of the division" between Germans East and West. And as if that weren't enough, he called it a "fashionable notion of political masturbation."[51]

In fact, that fashion appeared to be over for good when Germany was unified in 1990. Habermas himself called for a referendum on unification to make all Germans affirm the new democratic order and to strengthen constitutional patriotism. There were also calls for a proper constitutional convention. Yet, in the end, East Germany acceded to the Federal Republic on the basis of a clause in the existing West German Basic Law; no major revisions were made to the Constitution after years of deliberation by a constitutional commission. Many intellectuals—not all of them nationalists, by any means—thought that with the "anomaly" of the division gone, the Germans would now form a "normal" national consciousness. An artificial construction like constitutional patriotism—the "patriotism for professors"—could be safely discarded.

Yet, as it turned out, the history of constitutional patriotism was far from over: it was imported into Spain, for instance, and often misused as part of a wide-ranging debate on regional autonomy and asymmetrical federalism; it's been discussed as an overarching form of civic loyalty that can accommodate claims for cultural recognition in a country like Canada; and, as said at the beginning, it's been proposed as a way to conceive "European unity." I don't want to tell this transnational conceptual history here—a history that has involved its fair share of unfortunate misunderstandings and deliberate mistranslations. Rather, I now want to turn to the question of whether we can formulate *any* kind of general theory of constitutional patriotism—irrespective, for the moment, of conceptual pasts, particular applications, and potential future contexts.

Two

NATIONS WITHOUT QUALITIES?

Toward a Theory of Constitutional Patriotism

[A]s soon as, behind the country, there stands
the old State, justice is far away. In the modern
form of patriotism, justice hasn't much of a
part to play, and above all nothing is said which
might encourage any relationship between
justice and patriotism to be drawn.
—Simone Weil, *The Need for Roots*

THE PREVIOUS CHAPTER has suggested that
critics who see Habermas's (and, by implication,
Sternberger's) conceptions of constitutional patriotism as an answer to particular German challenges do
indeed have a point. Yet to claim that a concept was forged
in a particular place and at a particular time is of course
not to invalidate it or to suggest that it's unfit to travel.

In this chapter, I'd like to broaden the discussion and
see whether there can be anything like a general account
of constitutional patriotism. I first want to sketch an out-
line of the elements that, in my view, any theory of constitutional patriotism needs to contain. In particular, it
seems to me that every such theory ought simply first of
all to clarify its overall *purpose*. What is the question, in
other words, to which constitutional patriotism is sup-

posed to be the answer? After all, we can't take for granted that we need such theories in the first place.

In addition, every theory should provide an account of what I shall call the *object of attachment*, the *mode of attachment*, and the *reasons for attachment*. Related to the first in particular, there's also what one might name a requirement of *specificity*: why, in other words, should those committed to universal principles attach themselves to one polity rather than another? Finally, a theory ought to answer questions about the precise motivational (and, if you like, emotional) *consequences* of constitutional patriotism. Are we in the end talking about a kind of "reasonable loyalty," as some have suggested, about some sort of tempered pride or about other kinds of emotions altogether? What political mentality or persistent "structures of feeling" would characterize a people subscribing to constitutional patriotism?

At this point I need to stress a distinction that was already hinted at in the introduction: constitutional patriotism, I asserted there, is a *normatively dependent* concept. Therefore, what I need to do in this chapter in order to answer the questions posed in the above paragraphs—to fill in the blanks, if you like—is to sketch a moral background theory of fairness that renders my vision of constitutional patriotism *normative substantive*. That is, it's possible to think of a purely *positivist* notion of constitutional patriotism—broadly speaking, any enduring attachment on the part of citizens to persisting political arrangements (irrespective of any orientation toward human rights and democracy). A *moral* reading of constitutional patriotism, however, needs a background theory of what renders political arrangements legitimate, and that is what will be provided in this chapter. Note, however, that one could formulate other background theories to constitutional patriotism, ones that argue for different accounts of fairness or justice; I've tried here to provide the strongest moral reading of constitutional patriotism I can think of, but others might formulate stronger ones, or perhaps will find good reasons to settle for weaker background theories.

I also said at the outset of this essay that a general theory of constitutional patriotism should be clear about its own limits. Constitutional patriotism is of course not by itself some kind of civic panacea in cases of collective political breakdown; but more importantly, I'll argue—no doubt disappointingly for some—that constitutional patriotism at least to some extent has to rely on already existing political units: it is not a free-standing theory of political boundary-formation, and therefore does not answer questions about political self-determination which rival theories like liberal nationalism might well be in a position to answer (even if those answers turn out to be unsatisfactory, from a normative and practical point of view). Likewise, constitutional patriotism cannot by itself generate large degrees of social solidarity, as some proponents of the concept have claimed; rather, social solidarity will depend on how strong an interpretation of the underlying idea of fairness can take hold in a particular political culture.

These two rather defeatist conceptual concessions might make you want to ask: so what, then, is the point of constitutional patriotism? In short, constitutional patriotism, as set out in this chapter, *is* capable of avoiding the "sources of moral danger" associated with both liberal nationalism and traditional forms of patriotism—this is its distinctive virtue. It serves *both* as a source of civic trust (and therefore stability) *and* as a source of civic empowerment; it is inherently, to repeat a metaphor already suggested in the introduction, Janus-faced. The strong moral reading of constitutional patriotism outlined here always (and not contingently, as with liberal nationalism) contains what we might call a "normative surplus" that serves as a basis for civic empowerment, dissent, and—at the limit and as a kind of litmus test—as a justification for civil disobedience.[1] Polities subscribing to constitutional patriotism strengthen their defenses against illiberal and antidemocratic challenges, but they also willingly render themselves vulnerable to what we might call "normative disturbances" that derive their power from constitutional patriotism's normative surplus.

This normative surplus can also be invested, so to speak, in the mutual opening of constitutional cultures, and therefore is conducive to what I shall call, mixing metaphors freely now, "normative spillover" and a process of "transnational norm-building"—whereas liberal nationalism contingently might or might not have this feature. This "normative spillover" is another advantage constitutional patriotism has over its philosophical competitors, a claim that obviously depends on the desirability of such transnational norm-building—a stance I cannot fully justify within the scope of this essay, but one for which I shall try to provide at least some reasons toward the middle of this chapter.

Having set out a general theory of constitutional patriotism that relies on a strong moral theory as its backdrop, I'll attempt to show that such a theory can meet two objections which to me seem particularly important, as they do not simply replay the familiar chorus of "it's too abstract" or "not enough blood in it for me": the claim that constitutional patriotism is a form of "statist nationalism," and the suspicion that it amounts to a kind of "civil religion"—both of which could plausibly be construed as posing "moral dangers."

Finally, I want to descend from the heights of normative abstraction and ask what constitutional patriotism might mean as policy. Would it have the same practical consequences as liberal nationalism, or "civic nationalism"—a term which has yet to be distinguished from constitutional patriotism? Are all these concepts ultimately interchangeable abstractions, insofar as similar policies could be derived from them? How would one even recognize a "constitutionally patriotic polity"? Could we designate a polity as such, given certain criteria, when the leaders and citizens of that polity don't actually use the words "constitutional patriotism"? How, in other words, will we know it when we see it?

What's the Point of a Theory of Constitutional Patriotism? Some Sociological Doubts

Constitutional patriotism is not itself a theory of justice. It is also not primarily a theory of the self, even if the notion of post-conventional identity plays an important role in Habermas's conception of constitutional patriotism. Rather, as Frank Michelman has pointed out, constitutional patriotism is part (and *only* part) of a response to the challenge of conceiving, justifying, and maintaining democratic political rule—with the proviso that a successful justification will in turn make for the just and stable exercise of political rule.[2] Constitutional patriotism is not itself that justification, but justification will yield what I have already referred to as the "reasons for attachment."

Put differently: a theory of constitutional patriotism provides a language for exercises in what you might call "collective ethical self-clarification." Who and how do we want to be, as far as political rule over ourselves is concerned? Do we see such rule centered on some kind of cultural essence that should be preserved over time? Or do we conceive it as a project that sustains, and is in turn enriched by, a set of political conversations about the principles that should govern political rule?

Constitutional patriotism conceptualizes the beliefs and dispositions required for citizens to maintain a particular form of political rule. Now, the assumption that such beliefs and dispositions are required in the first place is hardly uncontroversial: an even not particularly harsh critic might say that we don't live in fifteenth-century republican Florence; that it is sociologically naïve to think that modern, highly complex societies are in any way "held together" by patriotic dispositions; and that, on a normative plane no less than an empirical one, the very language of patriotism perpetuates a profoundly problematic picture of society as a top-down-affair where elites decree beliefs and dispositions, instead of letting men and women get on with their lives. Advocates of patriotism, the not-too-harsh critic might go on to say, simply haven't understood that, in political thought no less than in the modern social imagination, we need to cut off the king's head.

Well, it's hard to dispute the claim that we don't live in fifteenth-century Florence, and that political attention and political care are scarce resources under contemporary conditions. But, again, it's also strangely unrealistic, as some highly sophisticated social theories want to make us believe, that complex societies effectively now run by themselves. Why, we might ask then, do we still see, again and again, prolonged, passionate, and sometimes extremely bitter disputes about precisely the kinds of ques-

tions to which constitutional patriotism is at least one
possible answer: questions about collective self-understandings; questions about membership, that is, who be-
longs in the first place; questions about the rights and
duties associated with citizenship, and the criteria for access to citizenship; and, finally, the dispositions and vir-
tues that might be necessary to have decent, let alone just,
regimes survive over time.[3] Perhaps participants in such
disputes (and I am not claiming that at any one point there
are ever more than tiny minorities that engage such questions in the public sphere) are all sociologically naïve. But
again, this supposedly realist view seems itself strangely
unrealistic, given that such disputes appear to have very
real legal and political consequences: citizenship laws do
change; rights and duties associated with membership status are redefined; and, not least, the moral imagination of
how different political collectives stand in relation to one
another can be profoundly transformed.

In short, there's no knock-down argument for why a
social theory that would make us dispense with patriotism
talk is utterly wrong. But there is enough nationalism and
patriotism talk already out there to make us want to think
about which vision of a collective self-understanding best
fits deeper moral concerns about justice and fairness. I'll
turn to that enterprise now.

Objects for Attachment: On Universal Norms and Constitutional Culture

The deepest impulse animating a normatively substantive
account of constitutional patriotism is the idea of individuals recognizing each other as free and equal and finding
fair terms of living together; in other words, to find

enough common, mutually acceptable grounds to answer the question, "How do want to live together?" In a sense, you might say, it's nothing less than the political question as such.

The seemingly innocuous phrase "living together" has larger implications than one might think at first: it means that constitutional patriotism refers necessarily to particular, more or less clearly bounded political associations. Its focus is on particular, pre-existing political structures, not humanity as a whole. However, it would be unjustified to jump to the conclusion that constitutional patriotism is therefore necessarily "statist," an accusation I'll come back to later in this chapter.

To spell out further what I have just called the deepest normative impulse: political rule—that is, the ground rules for the collective exercise of force over the members of the political community—ought to be justified to those subject to collective decisions. Otherwise, some citizens will simply dominate others. However, the need for justification does not apply to every single law or measure; rather, the system of lawmaking in general—or the "law of law-making"—and the principles animating it have to be justifiable to all citizens. In other words, for citizens to accept situations when they find themselves in a minority, they have to have endorsed what John Rawls once called "constitutional essentials." In particular, they have to endorse the general procedures that are presumed to produce legitimate law. Thus, according to Michelman,

> specific exercises of coercive political power are justified when they are validated by a set of constitutional essentials . . . that everyone can see that everyone has reason to accept in the light of his or her interests . . . , considering himself or herself to be one among a company of pre-

sumptively free and equal co-inhabitants, all of whom are
under moral motivational pressure to find agreement on
fair terms of cooperation within their necessarily shared
social space.[4]

Citizens are asked, then, to attach themselves to and
maintain a system of rules for law-making that tracks their
interests and that they would have no good reason to reject. It's on such a basis that ordinary laws and ordinary
politics, but also reasonable disagreements about particular interpretations of the constitution itself, should be acceptable even to those who find themselves in a minority.
Ordinary law will then at least have an indirect justification; it is produced by way of directly justified legal procedures defined in the constitution, and is therefore presumed to be legitimate.

Michelman has argued persuasively that citizens have
to be attached, in the first place, to the very *idea* of a constitution—or, if one wanted to rephrase this in order not
to keep overburdening the notion of "constitution," the
idea of committing oneself to mutual justification in a
well-ordered society with fair terms of cooperation and
fair terms of limiting power. That is, citizens are not asked
to agree on or accept a particular constitution in all its
specificity at a particular point in time; this would also be
an unreasonably restrictive *positivist* notion of constitutional patriotism. It is perfectly reasonable for citizens to
disagree even about some constitutional essentials (and
not just their application, for instance). Such disagreement will be likely not least, since a general justification,
on the one hand, and application, on the other, can almost
always not be properly separated: citizens will not be able
to foresee the outcomes of particular applications, and

they'll also in many instances have good reasons to disagree about how to translate constitutional essentials into
actual legal and political institutions. Constitutions will
serve as the site of intense and yet reasonable moral and
political contestation, not least in light of the core idea of
fairness that is as yet imperfectly realized in any given,
really existing constitution.

Constitutions, then, necessarily produce a form of contained disagreement or limited diversity. What contains
and limits here is again the attachment to the very idea of
citizens conceiving each other as free and equal should
find fair terms of political cooperation that they can justify to each other. It is this critical, and admittedly highly
abstract, idea that constitutional patriots have to adhere
to through thick and thin. And yet it's not at all irrelevant
that citizens have such an "abstract and critical demo-
cratic-constitutional orientation to the systems of cooperation in which they find themselves"; as James Tully has
put it, they at least share "a mode of problematisation
of their political identity."[5] Political situations look very
recognizably different where such a mode is absent,
where fair cooperation or even just somehow trying to
share a political space have ceased to be common goals.

It's on this still rather abstract level that constitutional
patriotism enters the picture. In (inevitable) cases of reasonable disagreement, constitutional patriotism will provide minorities with a genuinely moral motivation to
maintain the constitutional regime as a whole. After all,
they have reason to maintain a system which is supposed
to embody the ideal of mutual justification, even if—in
all likelihood—no individual citizen at any one point will
judge the embodiment of this idea in all its specificity congruent with his or her conception of fairness. Citizens

who find themselves in a minority might not always see that the system as a whole is in their interest when they feel that they have lost out on what for them is an important issue. In such cases, constitutional patriotism exerts additional moral pressure to uphold the system; it furnishes minorities with good, normative reasons to give what political scientists sometimes call "losers' consent."

At the same time, constitutional patriotism also provides minorities with a language to contest majority decisions, when they feel they have been treated unjustly. In other words, constitutional patriots in a minority will have a way of appealing to the majority's attachment to principles of fairness—in which case the majority cannot simply dismiss the minority as those whose self-interests have lost out with particular decisions. For instance, minorities can try to tell stories about ever widening circles of inclusion, appealing to a common patriotic care to remain faithful to constitutional essentials and render their realization "ever more perfect." In that sense, constitutional patriotism is also part of an account of the sources of the long-term stability of constitutional regimes—it provides a common language, or a mode of political problematization or contestation within a shared normative framework.

From specific debates and even disagreements about the constitution eventually emerges what some have termed a "constitutional identity," but what I'd prefer to call a "constitutional culture."[6] "Identity," in my view, suggests too static a picture, and tends to narrow the focus to an actual written document, the original of which we can see behind an exhibition glass, whereas "culture" points to the fact that we ought to include shared symbols, rites and rituals of membership, and venerated institutions, such as constitutional courts, that are associated with and, at least partially, express constitutional essentials. But it might also be something more abstract—such as certain practices of conducting debate in a public and civilized manner—that could come to characterize a constitutional culture; such situated practices would then also demand support from constitutional patriots.

Constitutional culture is not as expansive a term as "political culture"; at the same time it might turn out to be more, not less, particular than "political culture," even if the constitution itself, in line with Habermas's initial conception of constitutional patriotism, is seen as characterized, above all, by what we take to be or have negotiated as universal norms. After all—to say what for sociologists in particular will appear as the obvious—constitutions do not interpret or apply themselves; they are read and reread in light of particular historical experiences, new information, mutual learning across borders. And so on.

The term "culture," as opposed to "identity," also underlines that we're not dealing with something homogeneous or necessarily harmonious. Constitutional cultures are at least partly defined by the very nature of ongoing disagreements and deep-seated conflicts within a general constitutional settlement, and yet characteristic forms of conflict and difference still refer to the same thing—and, as political theorists from (pick your genealogy) Machiavelli to Albert Hirschman have argued, contained conflict can in fact also have an integrating and stabilizing effect.[7] A constitutional culture, then, will be characterized by certain styles of political claim-making and contestation, as well as ways of (at least temporarily) agreeing to disagree. In other words, conflict perceived

as legitimate can be as important as consensus for a particular constitutional culture.

But Is It *Ours*? The Specificity Requirement

Let us return to the question about the general structure
and content of a theory of constitutional patriotism posed
at the beginning: what is the overall purpose of constitutional patriotism? In a nutshell: to enable and uphold a
just constitutional regime. And, further, what is the object
for constitutional patriotism? The object of attachment is
not the (written or unwritten) constitution in all its concrete, historical specificity, as a positivist rendering of
constitutional patriotism would have it. Rather, it is ultimately the very idea of citizens mutually justifying political rule to each other—and thus, in the end, the moral
intuition that things should not just be done *to* people.
Constitutional patriotism contests any conception of
common life as a matter of "who, whom"—to use Lenin's
(perhaps shortest ever) definition of power as domination.

More specifically, citizens attach themselves to the
norms and values at the heart of the constitution, that is,
the constitutional essentials, and, in particular, the fair
and democratic procedures that can be presumed to produce legitimate law. Habermas has stressed time and
again that complex modern societies cannot be sustained
by a "substantive consensus on values but only by a consensus on the procedure for the legitimate enactment of
laws and the legitimate exercise of power."[8] Yet it's important to bear in mind that even in this picture universal
moral norms remain the ultimate source of attachment:
it is simply that they have "retreated" into the particular

procedures that structure the rules for reworking a constitutional culture.

So far, I've offered a preliminary answer to the question about the object of patriotic attachment. Yet if what has been said so far about universal norms and values is correct, constitutional patriotism would clearly not fulfill any specificity requirement. Men and women might simply decide to attach themselves to whichever regimes they find best embody the constitutional essentials they deem most important. However, the specificity requirement is fulfilled once we enlarge the "object of attachment" to include what above I have referred to as a "constitutional culture." The kinds of conversations and disagreements that characterize constitutional cultures are necessarily related to particular national and historical contexts. These contexts enter the judgments citizens make about the constitution and the forms of reasonable disagreements that can emerge. But the norms included in the constitution in turn will transform the way in which citizens view their traditions and the local, regional, and national cultures (not that any of these could be neatly separated) with which they find themselves confronted. Constitutional culture, one might say, at the very least mediates between universal norms and particular contexts. One might also say that constitutional culture itself is then formed through what could be envisioned as a circular process, in which constitution, constitutional culture, and a diverse and evolving set of cultural (including national) self-understandings in a more general sense come to influence and, ideally, reinforce one another.

Even constitutional patriots, then, do not come from nowhere. They find themselves entangled in—and hopefully thriving on—particular cultures, and, above all, face, sustain, and re-work particular constitutional cultures which are trying to express universal norms of justice and fairness in specific contexts. The best means to be faithful to universal norms and to render them actionable is to enter and enrich the ongoing conversation about a given political culture; and constitutional patriots remain faithful to the conversation not least by keeping faith with the ongoing disagreements which might characterize that conversation.

So constitutional patriotism *is* specific, and it is in any case an illusion, or an illegitimate appropriation, to think "the universal" can somehow be accessed directly or claimed in some incontestable manner—instead of being earned in conversation and negotiated and contested. Even in its specificity, however, constitutional patriotism remains primarily an attachment to norms or principles. What makes constitutional patriotism different from other forms of attachment is that it is not a group of people or a culture tout court that claims allegiance. Constitutional patriotism, one might say, is meant to be political through and through: people and "culture" become relevant only to the extent that they have an impact on politics, or, more specifically, the ground rules for the collectively authorized exercise of coercion.

Attachment and Agency: All Ambivalence?

Having clarified the object and the specificity of constitutional patriotism, let me move on to the other elements that in my view are needed for a general account. In particular, the question about the mode of attachment has yet to be answered. In moral-psychological terms, the mode of attachment might perhaps best be defined as reflective, critical, or sometimes even ambivalent. Constitutional essentials and constitutional culture more widely are all viewed in a critical light, and are subject to periodic evaluation and re-evaluation in light of what citizens take to be universal norms.

Constitutional patriotism is supposed to be reflexive. In other words, constitutional patriotism itself has occasionally to be revised and refined in light of the further development and refinement of the principles at the heart of our constitutional regime. In that sense, it could also be called, again drawing on a very Habermasian concept, a "collective learning process":[9] it presumes an open future and the willingness of citizens to adjust the reasons, the object, and the mode of their attachment in light of new experiences. Consequently, citizens see their constitutional culture as always *open* and *incomplete*—a project, in short, in which we can recognize those in the past as having been engaged and in which we would want our descendants to invest.[10]

We know practically that polities cannot live in permanent states of self-questioning and ambiguity. The (highly stylized) point is about a basic attitude toward politics that at least sometimes calls for intense critical attention. We cannot in advance say what these demanding moments will be like, what might trigger them, and whether "collective learning" might under certain conditions not go wrong—and lead to a "collective unlearning." But it's hardly trivial to make this point, as conceptions of constitutional patriotism centered on a static "constitutional identity," or forms of liberal nationalism that, with all due hedging, tend to rely on a core ethnic identity, would not necessarily frame the picture this way.[11]

As far as reasons for attachment are concerned, I've already indicated that citizens who seek to treat each other as free and equal in a common social space have reasons to adopt the principles of constitutional democracy. They also have reasons to sustain a struggle for the best realization of these principles through the course of reasonable disagreements. Clearly, there are more or less strict versions of this argument, depending on the moral background theory adopted. In a more strictly Kantian version, for instance, reasons for attachment could be construed exclusively as duties to uphold a just political order;[12] in a different version which stresses the importance of democracy for individual dignity, there might be instrumental reasons to sustain a constitutional culture or identity which allows for collective agency and collective learning processes. In other words, the reasons for attachment are not always the same, depending on one's particular moral background theory.

Now, does any of this imply that attachment has to be entirely rational? The question needs to be considered, not least because liberal-nationalist critics have made so much of the supposed "rationalism," "abstractness," and—inevitably, it seems—"bloodlessness" of the concept. It's fair to say that within constitutional patriotism as a form of attachment cognitive elements will predominate. But the symbolic contents of a constitutional culture, its narratives and projections into the future, will also evoke particular emotions. In fact, it will in all likelihood evoke a rather complex set of emotions—as opposed to simple pride, for instance.[13] Shame, righteous indignation (or what Habermas has at one point called "democratic indignation"), spiritedness, anger, and guilt might play more of a role than other emotions or passions commonly included in accounts of belonging.[14] These emotions, however, will necessarily depend on "cognitive antecedents": it's a mistake not to recognize that cognition and emotion are intimately related—emotions (or at least the ones of concern in political life) are, after all, based on beliefs.[15]

The moral life of constitutional patriots, then, is potentially rather complex, which is not to say that it is somehow *uniquely* complex. Liberal nationalists, partly because of what is often seen as the contradiction at the heart of the concept of liberal nationalism, might be as troubled, or even tormented. At the same time, it would be wrong to claim that constitutional patriotism involves a standard set of emotions and passions. What is certainly *not* compatible with the picture of a complex post-traditional society, however, is the presence of unquestioned pride and linear or homogeneous national narratives of heroes and victories.[16] In that sense, a post-traditional constitutional culture is indeed also a post-heroic one. And, as said before, it is post-nationalist, rather than post-national (and also post-*traditionalist*, for that matter).[17] After all, the constitutional culture remains not only based on, but also permeable to, national (and sub-national) experiences, and in particular narratives of troubling pasts, of oppression and oppression overcome.

Finally, there is what I posed earlier as a question about the results or the "product" of constitutional patriotism. Habermas has described these as "an abstract, legally mediated solidarity between strangers." This is certainly a far cry from Aristotelian or Florentine civic friendship, arising in a society of face-to-face political contacts. Yet it's not clear whether "solidarity" is quite the right term here. In the account I've offered so far, it is not obvious whether citizens are truly asked to make any sacrifices for each other in the sense of maintaining an extensive welfare state. In an indirect way one could argue that the fair value of the rule of law and democracy, and, in particular, the ideal of a public sphere open for deliberation from diverse points of view, needs resources that citizens must be willing to render to each other. Depending on the context, constitutional patriotism might support constitutional essentials that include very extensive redistribution of resources indeed. In itself, however, constitutional patriotism is not in any straightforward way a plank of support for a large welfare state.

Even with this limit, however, one might conclude that constitutional patriotism simply paints too irenic a picture of the political world; where do questions of inclusion and exclusion enter? If they don't enter at all, isn't constitutional patriotism potentially a sort of philosophical sedative that makes us put up with unexplained and unjustified inclusions and exclusions? It is here that the issue of motivational sources for agency and the question of loyalty intersect. Loyalty, by definition partial and relational, is said always to attach to a "historical self."[18] In other words, it is supposed to refer to a smaller or larger group of people (or perhaps just one loved person), and it appears to presume a shared history with particular people (or a person). Moreover, it is always exercised in the face of some threat, or, more precisely, another potential object of allegiance. In other words, what tests loyalty is the availability of some possibly quite attractive alternative—another person, another party, or perhaps another country. If that is the case, one is naturally led to ask with George Fletcher, "[H]ow might one be disloyal to the Constitution? There is no alternative lurking in the wings. It would make no sense for an American judge to consider applying the German or the Canadian constitution."[19]

To answer this challenge, one might first of all draw a distinction between two different kinds of loyalties. Simply put, one is loyalty to people, the other is loyalty to principles. Now, in practice, this distinction will often be blurred. Let's say, for instance, that we have engaged with others in a common effort in the past—a successful political struggle for greater justice and civic inclusion. What participants in that struggle might feel attached to is not just the principles of justice and inclusion, but also other participants, with whom we now share a history, and it is in all likelihood also the actual outcome of the struggle— for example, particular kinds of political institutions devoted to justice or a change in political mentalities. However, just as much as the distinction can be blurred, these two kinds of loyalty might also come into conflict. People we care about might behave in ways, or even develop in ways, that violate principles we care about. The main point, however, is that it is simply not the case that "the gears of loyalty simply do not engage the Constitution."[20] Principles can call for loyalty as much as people.

A better objection than saying that there is no "alternative in the wings" would be to claim that if we *only* care about principles, we might as well leave a country whose constitution is developing in such ways that the principles in question are being violated. In other words, the real issue is how much loyalty depends on any kind of shared history, as Fletcher claims. The answer, taking off from the earlier discussion about constitutional culture, would seem to me to be something like the following: even universal principles are of course embodied in particular institutions and practices, and we can become attached to these institutions without thereby automatically turning into particularists. These particular institutions and practices then *also* have meaning for us by virtue of our attach-

ment, and our involvement in the shared history of supporting, criticizing, and revising them.[21] As Joseph Raz
has put it, "[M]eaning comes through a common history,
and through work. They make the objects of one's attachment unique."[22] So it's possible, conceptually and empirically, to be attached to universalist principles *and* feel loyalty to a particular constitutional culture.

Why should all this be terribly important? A not unreasonable one-word answer would be "McCarthyism."
Any discussion of loyalty and the constitution is haunted
by the specter of political witch-hunts of those suspected
of lacking "political loyalty" or "civic reliability." Proponents of cultural nationalism have felt especially tempted
to oppose uncomplicated belonging by virtue of culture
to membership based on achievement or oath. The latter, it is then often claimed, does not allow for a genuine
sense of "being at home," as belonging will be dependent
on potentially changing standards of political behavior.
Paradoxically, then, the unchosen (birth or culture, let's
say) make for *political* freedom and enable tolerance
(think of an idealized version of Britain, tolerant of political eccentricities)—whereas the possibility of political
choice makes for exclusion (think of the United States
and McCarthyism).

I am not sure that this argument can be trumped in any
easy manner. It does presume culturally homogeneous
entities (otherwise fragmentation and the possibility of
exclusion reenter). And it does presume that the political
expression of these cultural entities will not have limits
to *cultural* tolerance. But this in itself is of course not
an argument for exclusively *political* identities instead. In
fact, we might simply have to admit that there is no guarantee that constitutional cultures will not turn out to be

intolerant. But by the same token, it's hardly inevitable that political forms of belonging will cash out as the need for loyalty oaths. In any case, the more heterogeneous societies become, the less we have a choice not to give citizens a choice and instead to stick with an expectation of cultural conformity.

There is a further, theoretical response to anxieties about McCarthyism—without this being a guarantee either. After all, constitutional patriotism itself—at least in the way I have presented it—refers us back to the core idea of citizens recognizing one another as free and equal. It is hard to see that constitutional cultures built around this idea could ever become so perverted that they encourage systematic intolerance, but it's not impossible, of course. What needs to be stressed, though, is that the self-critical and the reflective are, in the strong moral reading suggested here, built into the very notion of constitutional cultures that constitutional patriotism is supposed to sustain as a form of post-conventional, post-traditionalist, post-nationalist belonging. Such a constitutional patriotism finds the normative resources for contestation *within itself*—it has recourse to the very grounds of the constitutional essentials that are being violated. In short, it is *reflexive*.

On the Limits of Constitutional Patriotism, and on Comparisons with Liberal Nationalism

As I've indicated at the outset, it's important to stress what constitutional patriotism does not provide: in particular, it's not in itself a theory to determine political boundaries. In this regard, one might say, it shares a weakness of liberal thought more generally, that of, by and large, taking for granted existing bounded political space. Certainly no demand for cultural self-preservation by means of political autonomy could be deduced from the theory. It's true that constitutional patriotism makes a claim for the de-centering and mutual opening of existing constitutional cultures. In that sense—very, very broadly speaking—it is more likely to come down on the side of political arrangements that integrate rather than separate. But this is only a relatively weak guideline. It's certainly conceivable in theory that a national minority, faced with unbearable oppression, sets up its own state, institutes a constitutional regime, and makes a point of critically re-working its own traditions. In other words, there is nothing necessarily contradictory about a group of politically self-determining post-nationalists. So, unlike what critics have claimed, constitutional patriotism can offer an account of political continuity by virtue of its focus on constitutional cultures. But it can't offer a full-fledged account of political demarcation.

Having said that, constitutional patriotism is compatible with—in fact, encourages—what I have referred to at the outset as "transnational norm-building." By this rather ugly neologism I mean the emergence of ever more complex political and moral ties across state borders—without these ties making state borders superfluous or morally insignificant—as well as practices of mutual learning and mutual deliberative engagement. Constitutional patriotism, on account of its commitment to universal norms, will be conducive the formation of such ties. However, since it recognizes legitimate differences among constitutional cultures, it will not collapse into a version of monist cosmopolitanism: that is, a cosmopolitanism that considers political boundaries morally irrelevant and assumes that all human beings stand in exactly the same moral-political relation to one another.

Now at first sight one might object that, rather paradoxically, constitutional patriotism could precisely block such mutual engagement—because "we" want jealously to protect "our" constitution, and not have "our" constitutional judges cite foreign law and import other people's constitutional essentials; and that, if anything, a strong emphasis on constitutions as a focus of political belonging could easily foster a kind of narcissism of minor constitutional differences. But such *constitutional nationalism*—or, in Frank Michelman's more benign formulation, constitutional "integrity anxiety"—clearly does violence to the understanding of constitutional patriotism advanced here: one that does not see constitutional cultures as fully "achieved" and closed to self-critical learning, but rather views them as an ongoing project of realizing certain norms and vales in an "ever more perfect" way.[23] At the same time, it leaves open the possibility of significant variations in constitutional cultures, even in constitutional essentials, but *after* a process of mutual engagement, and the weighing of other political possibilities, not as a dogmatic closing-off of a transnational discussion of norms and values on account of the stipulated self-sufficiency of national democratic self-government.[24]

Thus, constitutional patriotism recognizes the legitimacy of political morality being *multilayered*—and accepts the idea that bounded schemes of fair living together impose more stringent obligations than "the worldwide community of human beings."[25] It also values the fact that there are borders and existing bounded schemes of cooperation, but does so while hoping to transform such schemes in ever more liberal, just, and inclusive directions. Borders and schemes of cooperation are not simply obstacles, but also resources, or even, if you like, achievements (as exercises in state-building and nation-building from scratch keep sadly demonstrating). Constitutional patriotism attempts to conceive what we might call *fairness in the face of achieved institutions*, without assuming that institution can be normatively achieved and justified once and for all. This is no doubt one major concession to the political reality of a world already divided into states, and some might well see this as one crucial concession too many.

This element of political realism also has other, less defeatist implications, however.[26] In particular, constitutional patriotism, as suggested here, does not fall victim to what we might call the *foundationalist fallacy*: it simply doesn't claim, as has often been alleged by critics, that men and women have to come together ex nihilo, so to speak, to create a polity based on pristine universalist values: constitutional patriotism transforms, it doesn't create out of nothing. In the same vein, it doesn't fit what we might call the *rationalist-voluntarist fallacy*: in other words, it doesn't claim that attachment has to be purely rational and voluntary; again, it reshapes (or rather, we reshape) our dispositions and emotions, and does not depend on a completely unrealistic pure politics of will. Michelman has put the point rather poetically: "constitutional patriotism recovers and explains the possibility of moral reasons and of moral experience, but at the same time it shows them to be reasons and experience into which we always enter not in entire forgetfulness but trailing clouds of culture from our particular national home."

This also means that constitutional patriotism dispenses with the distinction between "good civic" and "bad ethnic" nationalism that sociologists have rightly called "conceptually ambiguous, empirically misleading, and normatively problematic."[27] Consequently, we also shouldn't call constitutional patriotism a fancy version of civic nationalism: it's a transformative conception of living together that is different from civic nationalism, and it does suggest a different moral psychology than nationalism of any sort, whether ethnic or civic.

But you might ask, is it not a severe limit that constitutional patriotism, while being a theory of the civic bond, does not tell us then how to generate social solidarity? Does liberal nationalism, which claims that members of the same nation are prepared to trust and to make sacrifices for one another, not have a distinctive advantage here, both as a normative and as an explanatory account? Don't we see evidence every day that people really are prepared to sacrifice for their nations—in fact, sacrifice everything and die for it? Whereas, on the other hand, we probably won't ever see the tomb of the unknown post-nationalist.

Unlike my position with regard to political boundary-formation, I'm not prepared to make any concessions here. To construe a conceptual link between nationalism and the welfare state, liberal nationalists have had to claim that solidarity is higher among those who feel themselves to be similar (or even the same) in some significant aspect. There is indeed some, but by no means conclusive, *empirical* evidence that ethnically homogeneous societies can sustain higher levels of redistribution. One possible *ethical* argument for the connection is to claim that nationality per se imposes obligations of welfare provision for less well-off co-nationals. In other words, just as identifying oneself as a member of a family entails certain responsibilities, the self-identification as a co-national is supposed to lead to certain obligations. Yet the "shared understanding," or even moral intuition, about family obligations is both much deeper and much, much more widespread than similar intuitions about nationality. "National solidarity" is a form of solidarity that is particularly vulnerable to large-scale changes in political culture and collective ethical self-understandings; in the end, an identity-based, instrumental argument for the welfare effects of nationalism remains historically highly contingent. It also, by the way, does not tell us how to get the right "national identity," if, that is, we don't already have it.

A potentially more persuasive argument holds that sacrifices for others within a shared national culture aren't sacrifices at all. Rather, according to this line of reasoning, the nation provides a larger sense of self, so that sacrifices are in fact not genuine acts of altruism. The ethical status of this argument remains obscure: in particular, it's not clear whether this sort of "enlarged egotism" constitutes an ethical argument at all. It's also dubious whether many of those coerced by nation-states to pay taxes for the purpose of redistribution in fact harbor such notions about a "larger self." And even if citizens understood themselves as part of a larger self, there is still the question how that larger self understands itself. In other words, the larger self, the nation, might have ideas about justice which do not translate into extensive redistribution. Once again, this thought simply puts justice at the mercy of changing "shared understandings" and mentalities.

Then there's the question of trust. Not to put too fine a point on it, for welfare provision to work one needs some reassurance that those who are supposed to give and those entitled to claim comply with the laws. Sanctions, so the argument holds, can go some way in ensuring compliance, but schemes for welfare provision will only function properly if citizens can trust each other. Trust, however, seems to stand in once more for sameness; in other words, only if citizens can assume that others are like them and, in particular, that they're like them in the significant aspect of being willing to show solidarity with co-nationals. Thus one is back to the issue of whether the particular sameness, or identity, in question generally encourages solidarity or not. This is of course not to claim that trust doesn't matter for a successful politics. But is it not more plausible to say that trust derives from a shared political project, from caring and being concerned about that project—and that trust then in turn supports that project? In other words, it's real practices and actually shared activity, such as the maintenance and furtherance of a constitutional culture, that generate political identity, not a supposedly given, reified "national culture."

But the most important objection to this whole liberal-nationalist line of reasoning is arguably this: it's not too much of a historical generalization to say that welfare states have come about as a result of political *struggles* for participation and justice. Rarely, if ever, has "communal solidarity" created "a feeling, or an illusion, of closeness and shared fate, which is a precondition of distributive justice."[28] Rather, sometimes some people have persuaded or even forced others to recognize that they share a fate and therefore are well-advised to participate in schemes of redistribution. The habit of participating in such schemes might then eventually also engender feelings of "communal solidarity." Movements for social justice,

however, have hardly ever relied on *national* rhetoric; welfare states have been the outcome of political battles (or
states' attempts to preempt such battles). They are not
the results of men (indeed, men) generously extending
fellow-feeling.

In the end, liberal nationalism's claim about the motivational power of "the nation" seems so persuasive because we all can think of images of self-sacrifice that appear to be "national"—in war, particularly. But the
emotional power of such sacrifice is better understood if
we see "the nation" here for what it is on the battlefield:
a quasi-religious, transcendent abstraction, almost a mystical body linking the past, the present, and the future, or
indeed a little, very concrete platoon of family and friends
that one finds have to be defended. Such mystical nationalism or personal loyalty are, to say the least, a very different matter from the everyday willingness of citizens wanting to pay taxes for really existing strangers.

Two More Objections: Is Constitutional
Patriotism Statist, and Is It a Civil Religion?

Let me now deal with two important objections that—
rather than the usual theoretical wailing for more
"bloody" concepts—do not in principle doubt the motivational power of constitutional patriotism, but rather
converge on the claim that constitutional patriotism necessarily tends to become *illiberal*, irrespective of the universal, democratic norms and values that have been said
to be at its core. Put differently, constitutional patriotism
might not be able to avoid the normative and practical
pitfalls that tend to be associated with nationalism and

that in fact animate the criticisms of nationalism advanced by advocates of constitutional patriotism themselves.

The two objections to constitutional patriotism I have in mind can be formulated as follows: first, there is the claim that constitutional patriotism is in fact a form of "statist nationalism" and therefore ultimately tends to replicate the problems commonly associated with nationalism. As Joseph Weiler has put it when criticizing the proponents of a European constitutional patriotism, "to be a good constitutional liberal, it would seem from this idiom, is to be a constitutional nationalist and, it turns out, the constitutional stakes are not only about values and limitations of power but also about its opposite: the power which lurks underneath such values."[29] Second, while constitutional patriotism is not necessarily a variety of nationalism, it is—and this might be normatively and practically even worse—a form of "civil religion"; that is, broadly speaking, a form of collective self-worship in the extreme case, or at least an ideology that makes citizens venerate their constitution and their civic myths as quasi-transcendent objects.

Clearly, these objections operate on quite different philosophical-normative and empirical levels. However, they are both animated by a certain distrust of what one might call, for shorthand, an "identitarian logic." What I mean is this: constitutional patriotism is conceived as a form of "political identity" by critics espousing the objections mentioned above, and while not all the subsequent steps of reasoning are necessarily explicated, it supposedly follows that "identities" always exclude, and that they necessarily require, an "Other," if not an outright enemy. It's argued that "political values can be as effective markers of group identity and as exclusionary as ethnic allegiances," and that, furthermore, constitutional patriotism remains within the "national-statist tradition of citizenship."[30]

It's tempting to respond to these objections by redefining constitutional patriotism as *only* a form of *critique*. It might then become a means of "resisting identifications," rather than itself being a form of "identification"; it might also then more easily meet the normative demand to "facilitate the inclusion of, and the venturing toward, the other" that one critic of constitutional patriotism has advanced.[31] The "identitarian logic," so to speak, is simply disabled, as constitutional patriotism is no longer in any direct way about conceptualizing what citizens have in common; it's in fact rather about criticizing in the name of universalist norms and values what they have in common.

Now, it's indeed always possible to claim that constitutional patriotism has to serve primarily as critique, as long as constitutional patriotism as a fully normatively justified collective identity is not yet achieved. Or one might say that such a collective identity will never be achieved, and that a perfect match between normative aspirations and an actually existing constitutional culture—constitutional patriotic "closure," if you like, or perhaps the closing of what Samuel Huntington once called the "IvI" gap (that is, ideas versus institutions)—is both impossible and profoundly undesirable.[32] It then appears more plausible to say that since no actually existing constitution, or, more broadly, actually existing state structures, can ever live up to expectations drawn from a pristine universalism, critique inspired by constitutional patriotism is indeed a form of *permanent* critique that will never result in anything like an unproblematic civic identification with an existing polity. Such a *lack* of closure will at the same time provide an incentive to continue struggling for an ever fuller, and yet never full, realization of universalist ideals.

I've myself suggested precisely this picture of constitutional patriotism as centered on a project earlier on and I certainly don't want to renounce it here; but to *only* stress critique, it seems to me, is in fact too easy a way of meeting the objections listed at the outset. It tacitly presumes that other kinds of collective identities will persist against which constitutional patriotism as critique can work; and, on the basis of what seems a rather mechanistic model, it appears to imagine constitutional patriotism as an ongoing project of "purging" a political culture. That is, there is an essentially unargued premise that political stability is already ensured in some form or another; at the same time, there is the claim that every political culture will persistently be contaminated by illegitimate forms of particularism which will then have to be cleansed away in the name of constitutional patriotism. All this is only part of the story; it can't be the entire story. Or, if you like, this is only one face of constitutional patriotism, and constitutional patriotism, as I said earlier, is always Janus-faced.

So, with respect to the first objection, the idea that constitutional patriotism is in fact a form of statist nationalism relies on a distinction between cultural and political nationalism.[33] Cultural nationalism, the argument goes, assumes that those who share a "common history and societal culture have a fundamental, morally significant interest in adhering to their culture and in sustaining it across generations."[34] Political nationalism, on the other hand, refers to the idea that for states to realize political values such as justice, welfare, and perhaps even liberty, citizens of states ought to share a homogeneous national culture. As Chaim Gans has argued, statist nationalism designates "the position . . . according to which a common national culture is a condition or means for the realization of political values which neither derive from national cultures nor are intended for their protection."[35] Put simply, cultural nationalism takes culture as an end, whereas political nationalism takes culture as a means. According to this analysis—and at first sight not unreasonably—constitutional patriotism could be placed with statist nationalism.

It's important to recognize the force of the objection that can be derived from this distinction (I am not claiming that Gans himself derives an actual normative objection of the kind that I elaborate here). First, constitutional patriotism, to the extent that it is actually a form of civic attachment or political loyalty—and not a free-floating set of universalist beliefs—necessarily needs to be focused on a *state*. Second, to the extent that constitutional patriotism is focused on a particular polity and aims at the formation of a homogeneous political culture characterized by a common set of beliefs concerning norms and values, it's necessarily a form of nationalism.

Of course, the objection fails if, more or less by fiat, nationalism is defined as a purely cultural phenomenon. But, again, this would make things too easy. What the objection brings out is that, unless constitutional patriotism is understood purely as critique—in the sense explained above—it is necessarily statist and particular, in a way that might make it structurally no different from nationalism. *Historically*, patriotism is actually closer to "reasons of state" than the cultural nationalism that arose toward the end of the eighteenth century.[36] Critics might then be tempted to say that constitutional patriotism is simply civic nationalism, and civic nationalism is still nationalism of sorts, and not automatically less fraught with danger in contrast with cultural nationalism. In particular, it still aims at homogeneity among citizens in a way that would have been recognizable to an antiliberal like Carl Schmitt as allegedly indispensable for democracy, and that more or less directly imperils values such as inclusiveness, individuality, and diversity.

In my view, a defense of constitutional patriotism that effectively counters its equation with statist nationalism ought to look something like the following: it has to be underlined again that constitutional patriotism is in itself not a justification for a particular polity, let alone a panacea for ensuring political stability, the reason simply being that a normatively substantial concept of constitutional patriotism relies on the idea of *sharing political space on fair terms*. Constitutional patriotism cannot create the motivation to subscribe to such an idea ex nihilo, but it can make sense of a continuous commitment to it, and further such a commitment.

The main point is this, however: constitutional patriotism does not designate the homogeneity of individual beliefs, or of ascriptive or voluntary identities, which then simply serve the implementation of other political or social values. Constitutional patriotism, in the substantial normative version defended here, is valuable in itself and, rather than simply facilitating justice or other values, it actually conceptualizes the beliefs and dispositions of a citizenry committed to justice or other values (for instance in the form of the idea of sharing common political space under fair terms of cooperation). Nationalism— and, more precisely, "trust" on account of national sameness—is the means in ideologies that we might indeed call "statist nationalism"; it's not a good in itself (as opposed to the cultural nationalism that designates a cultural nation as a value in itself). Constitutional patriotism as here defined, on the other hand, cannot be separated from justice, or solidarity, and seen simply as a means.

Constitutional patriotism is therefore fundamentally different from the logic that underlies liberal nationalism to the extent that a liberal nationalism which uses a common culture as a means to social solidarity is in fact, according to Gans's typology, a form of statist nationalism. Constitutional patriotism, by contrast, is not primarily tied to a state, but to political principles, and has normative value in itself—even if it is not, as argued above, a full-fledged normative theory or justification. Thus, perhaps paradoxically, constitutional patriotism, rightly defined, is intrinsically good, and yet, as a concept, normatively dependent.

What, then, about the suspicion that constitutional patriotism is a form of civil religion? It might be helpful broadly to distinguish three ways of thinking about "civil religion." First, there is what one might call a strong religious version in which religion profoundly structures political life. The paradigmatic case of such a religious "structuration" of society has been elaborated by Marcel Gauchet;[37] any serious consideration of the question of "civil religion" should at the outset consider Gauchet's claim that such a total religious structuration of society is simply not available under modern conditions, after what Gauchet famously called the "exit from religion." And if such a structuration—or restructuration—is attempted under modern conditions, it will result in a form of totalitarianism.[38]

Second, there is the classic Rousseauean version that treats broadly defined religious beliefs, or "natural religion," or a *religion du citoyen*, as a means by which to render a certain kind of republican politics possible. It's the sentiment summed up by a twentieth-century Rousseauean who claimed: "Our government makes no sense unless it is founded on a deeply felt religious faith—and I don't care what it is." This, then, is an essentially *functionalist* view of religion, a view that treats religion instrumentally.

Third, there is the weaker, quasi-sociological claim in which civil religion denotes a more or less metaphorical invocation of concepts, dispositions, and behaviors associated commonly with religion; and, in particular, a view of such concepts, dispositions and behaviors as having been transferred from religious to political objects. Veneration of symbols such as flags, national anthems, pledges of allegiance, ceremonies at statesmen's tombs, "Constitution Days," even battleships named after the constitution—this, then, is the stuff of civil religion, in which "religion" is ultimately but a metaphor for the process of creating and reinforcing the "symbolic power" of constitutions.[39]

The division outlined here is obviously crude, but for my purposes it might be enough to say that it's clearly the third kind of civil religion that critics of constitutional patriotism are concerned with. We have to ask what, precisely, these normative concerns are and whether they're at all valid. I should like to distinguish two normative perils: on the one hand, attitudes of veneration—of the constitution, of the memory of historical events, of particular historical figures, or of *lieux de mémoire* specifically to do with the constitution—might encourage what one might call forms of "uncritical citizenship." It might well be true that "constitutions do not live by texts alone" and that "constitutional communities" always constitute "communities of memory and experience."[40] But different "communities" allow for very different levels of contestation and critique, and what Jean-Marc Ferry has termed "consensus through confrontation" is very different from consensus through cultic practices, or what Louis Hartz once called a "conformitarian ethos."

Patterns of constitutional veneration might encourage the strategic manipulation of such constitutional symbols by political elites, or a competition for "capturing" and "decontesting" the meaning of such symbols so as to discourage or, in the extreme, try entirely to disable political dissent. Short of such illiberal scenarios, it might generally be the case that "flurries of reverential activity," as occurred for instance in the United States in the 1920s, might be reliable indicators of deeper-seated, structural "problems of democracy" trying to work themselves out—in which case political theory, rather than provide theories about flurries, should presumably address these deeper problems.[41] That is to say, there might be a genuine trade-off between democratic contestation and constitutional veneration, and it's at least imaginable that constitutional patriotism perniciously reinforces the latter, rather than enabling the former.

On the other hand, there are the perils of "civic millenialism" and of what one might call "chosen-people syndrome," which, as John Pocock has shown, have so frequently been associated with republican politics.[42] From the perspective of social psychology, one might say, it's simply very hard to avoid the shift from a sacralization of one's own to a belief in the superiority of one's own, even if such a shift is in no way *conceptually* necessary. This missionary impulse, or, if you like, compulsive connecting to the religious imagination, then also comes to resemble many accounts of nationalism much more than the defensive or protective posture which, historically, has been associated with patriotic virtue.

One might easily conclude that the abstract principles of liberal-republican patriotism always seem in need of supplements of concreteness, or perhaps even concrete oppositions which yield the moral motivation to adhere to and fight for such principles. Here, we really do come close to the notion of patriotism as a kind of illiberal and anti-individualist "group-based meaningfulness" which Kateb has criticized, as well as the "connection between patriotism and militarized death" which Kateb has also highlighted. And indeed there can be little doubt that *historically* patriotism and ideas of self-sacrifice have been closely related: in particular, Christian ideals of self-sacrifice and *agape* were often transferred to a divinized *patria*; patriotism was spiritualized, and religion linked to reasons of state.[43]

Again, there is an easy way out—that is, a way of countering this suspicion about constitutional patriotism by definitional fiat—but then there's also a somewhat more complex rejoinder. The easy way out is in fact a return to the original Habermasian conception of constitutional patriotism: Habermas, you might recall, while locating his conception of constitutional patriotism in a broad republican tradition, did not think that an unproblematic return to a pre-national (and premodern) patriotism centered on civic friendship was possible. "Constitutional veneration" clearly is incompatible with what one might call an "orthodox" version of Habermasian constitutional patriotism. Of course, the critic might object, so much

the worse for the orthodox version of Habermasian constitutional patriotism, because we just can't do without
pride and friendship. And the critic might argue further
that for constitutional patriotism to become effective as a
form of moral motivation, the kinds of perilous supplements of particularity mentioned above are always likely
to come into play.

Let's grant the point for the moment. Let's just say that
consistent post-conventional and post-traditional sets of
beliefs and patterns of behavior simply cannot be main-
tained in the face of weakness of will, a craving for the
supposedly concrete, an overwhelming aesthetic desire
for symbolism and meaning in politics, the motivating
force and meaning-generating presence of enmity, or any
other reason of which critics of constitutional patriotism
might think.[44] The crucial point, then, is that constitutional patriotism—in its normatively substantive, not
purely positivist version—carries within itself the resources to counter and correct the perils and problems
associated with the third kind of civil religion. Clearly,
such corrections in particular might take time to have an
effect—in which case it might be too late for some who
have suffered from the "identitarian" illiberal dangers
that might be associated with constitutional patriotism.
But this is still better than, let's say, the politics of liberal
nationalism, which simply does not have any such in-built
corrective tendencies (assuming that liberal nationalism
really is nationalism, and not just national liberalism).

I've tried to suggest that the three somewhat more un-
conventional objections to constitutional patriotism,
which all point to the perils of an alleged "identitarian
logic" at the heart of constitutional patriotism, are certainly not without merit. Yet all can be effectively coun-

tered by drawing on the resources which a normatively rich conception of constitutional patriotism ought to contain. Such resources, I hasten to add, cannot *guarantee* that constitutional patriotism in practice will not turn illiberal and exclusionary. In the same vein, it cannot guarantee what, short of all-out illiberalism, has been painted as the specters of "*hoheitliches Integrationsmanagement*" [officially managing integration from above] through constitutional courts, or constitutional patriotism *par le haut*, where political elites decree constitutional values.[45] But I am not sure political and legal theorists who want guarantees really expect; nor am I sure of the expectations of those who, from the beginning, would want to rule out any "identity talk" for fear of "othering," or who drop a Schmittian "h-word" (here, homogeneity), as soon as there is any talk of allegiances, or even just political coalition-formation. Democratic politics *is* risky, and without guarantees, especially within a shared space of free and equal citizens who don't want their politics entirely guaranteed—or even ordered—by a state and who indeed do want to resist any management of group loyalties from above. Constitutional patriotism is a bet on the right civic attitudes within that shared space and even beyond; it's not an insurance policy.

Practical Constitutional Patriotism?

Let me finally turn to more concrete questions, not least to address the suspicion that "applied constitutional patriotism" might simply be liberal democracy of one variety or another, so far as institutions are concerned, and just a matter of more self-critical attitudes when it comes to what citizens themselves actually feel and think. In which case, why would one need the more or less grand theoretical apparatus proposed so far? In this section of the chapter I want to say something about what constitutional patriotism might imply practically, especially for the question of "integration," both of minorities and of societies at large. I'll turn to the separate problem of supranational integration in the third and final chapter.

Let me first of all make a broader point, though: it seems to me that there's only so much that can be said at a very general normative level about "integration": there is a core set of principles that liberal democracies must not violate; but beyond those, much will depend on the particular background histories and aspirations of the countries and minority groups in question, cultural belief systems, family and clan structures, and so forth. Saying, for instance, that "Muslim communities" across Europe have to be "integrated" in such and such a way assumes that knowing that those "to be integrated" are Muslims is the most important thing there is to know—as if the differences were not greater between a second-generation Turkish noncitizen and member of the middle class in Germany, whose father was a *Gastarbeiter*, and a second-generation French citizen, whose father was a *harki*, fighting the Algerian rebels alongside the French Army in the war of Algerian independence. Moreover, the very language of "integration" thus conceived suggests an image of human beings being moved, or pushed, around in large-scale, more or less high-minded schemes of social engineering—an image that further seduces its users to think that "boundaries" or "thresholds" can clearly be specified, so that humans are simply recognizable as above or below that "threshold," or as inside or outside the "national culture" which liberal nationalists cherish.

What can in general be said about "integration," in my view, is this: the core of the core set of principles, as far as integration is concerned, is fairness—the very idea which animates the strong moral reading of constitutional patriotism proposed in this chapter. What this means, above all, is that there is a prima facie case for civic inclusion for those who have lived and worked within a polity that understands itself as subscribing to constitutional patriotism. Thus, an interminable exclusion of *Gastarbeiter*, or of so-called illegal aliens—when it is clear that the human beings in question contribute to a bounded scheme of social cooperation—can't be permissible under the reading advocated here.

In turn, however, it is permissible that those to be included meet certain criteria—criteria that can be more clearly and more justly specified in a framework of constitutional patriotism than under the rubric of liberal nationalism, for instance. It is in my view wrong to see constitutional patriotism (as described here) and its expression in more concrete policies as inevitably contaminated with culture and ethnicity, and therefore as exclusionary in the way that, for instance, Dora Kostakopoulou has suggested.[46] It's perfectly true that citizenship tests by themselves will not ensure anything, and that integration, when understood as a "collective mental process," cannot "be ordered by law";[47] an environment where the contributions of immigrants and their descendants are properly recognized might indeed be far more important for integration and "identification" than a one-off testing of political knowledge, which, in any case, might say little about the actual political attitudes of an applicant for citizenship. Declarations of high-minded universalism will appear hypocritical at best, if not matched by a scheme of fair opportunities, and a culture of non-discrimination: this is arguably the tragedy of French Republicanism, which promises universal accessibility through the state and yet sees everyday discrimination in society—except that the state can't actually see it, because the ban on culturally and ethnically coded statistics renders the state blind and society illegible.

In the same way, the ability to speak the main language of a country is much more likely to contribute to integration than mastering a specific civic vocabulary. It's easy to be glib here, although the glibness can be found on both sides of the debate: advocates of compulsory language classes seem often to have no sense that it can be a difficult or even humiliating experience for grown-ups to be "sent back to school;" whereas opponents of language classes are far too quick to assume that there isn't a cost to conceiving polities as "communities of communities"—where those costs will be paid by those locked into specific communities because of a lack of linguistic (and also civic) capacities.

The main points are these: not all requirements or expectations beyond a simple procedure of civic registration send a signal of hostility; not everything that appears to affirm "identity" is therefore primarily designed to reinforce exclusion; not all political or even historical knowledge that might be seen as important for citizenship is automatically exclusionary on an ethnic basis—events, historical figures, and broader principles themselves might well become part of a larger narrative of inclusion. It all depends *how* it's done. There's much to be said for the view that "membership . . . is meaningful only when ac-

companied by rituals of entry, access, belonging, and privi-
lege."[48] No doubt such civic meaning making and capacity
building can look silly or excessively "modernist" in the
eyes of some. But it's not an obviously illegitimate demand.

To be sure, constitutional patriotism is not meant to be
a return to traditional—and rightly discredited—ideals
of assimilationism as cultural conformity that have often
been associated with civic nationalism (which in turn, as
has often been pointed out, is not in any way itself an
indicator of actual cultural openness, let alone socioeco-
nomic porousness). Constitutional patriotic "integration" is not simply code for absorption which in turn
might be code for assimilation which in turn might be
code for "acculturation"—in other words, precisely the
chain of unwarranted assumptions and expectations that
liberal nationalism tends to encourage. Rather, following
Rogers Brubaker, we might want to imagine a shift from
"transitive" to "intransitive" understandings of assimilation: integration not as something done to "them," but
something accomplished in common through mutual deliberative engagement (for the most part under state auspices), but above all "with them"—in such a way that a
reconstituted "we" emerges.[49] Integration thus understood is not normatively opposed to the value of difference or diversity, but practically meant to prevent marginalization and "ghettoization," and therefore contrasts,
above all, with "benign neglect."[50]

Let me finally suggest a number of indicators of how
we might detect an actually existing or a developing form
of constitutional patriotism—the thing, that is, not the
word. First, is a country's particular immigration regime
one that can broadly be classified as a "universal-source"
regime?[51] Or do ethnic preferences structure immigration

policies? Note that immigration does not necessarily have to be particularly liberal (in the sense of generosity of openness), although more openness would in itself also be an indicator of constitutional patriotism. Clear ethnic preferences, however, would generally be a very strong pointer toward liberal nationalism, where certain ethnic groups are seen as more easily "compatible" with the "national culture."

Second, are citizenship tests and rituals of membership focused on political values, or are they for the most part—whether explicitly or implicitly—about a "way of life," a national culture, or, if you like, a thicker *Sittlichkeit*? Obviously, it's hard to draw hard and fast distinctions here. Nevertheless, a preponderance of questions focused on high culture, or specific confrontations with highly specific segments of a way of life (as in the Dutch minister Rita Verdonk's infamous proposal to confront would-be immigrants to the Netherlands with images of gay couples kissing and bare-breasted women on Dutch beaches), might in fact point to liberal nationalism rather than constitutional patriotism (or to poor political judgment, of course).

Third, are tests and rituals of membership applied across the board of applicants? Inconsistencies here would again indicate liberal nationalism, or a form of republicanism that remains more or less secretly imbued with a particular national culture.[52] Take as an example here the attempt failed by some German states to apply certain kinds of tests only to applicants for citizenship from so-called Muslim countries.

Fourth, is public justification of immigration regimes and membership rights and duties oriented toward political values and constitutional essentials in particular?

Again, it will be difficult to draw hard and fast distinctions here, but there clearly is a difference between regimes that justify immigration through kinship, or economic benefits, or historical bonds and legacies.

Fifth, what is the legal approach to the de facto multi-culturalism of a given country, and, in particular, is it consistent across ethnic, religious, and cultural communities? For instance, is there a libertarian free-speech regime, or one that could be called "dignitarian" because, as in German and other types of continental European law, the dignity of collectives and their capacity to be insulted is explicitly recognized?[53] If so, is what appears as the majority culture subject to particular protection (in the way that, for instance, the Turkish Penal Code makes "insults to Turkishness" punishable?) The claim is not that one is necessarily a pointer toward constitutional patriotism, and the other away from it; rather, the question is about consistency, either of a libertarian or a dignitarian approach. Inconsistencies here would point toward liberal (or even illiberal) nationalism, rather than constitutional patriotism.

Sixth, in what way are immigrants and applicants for citizenship in particular expected to relate to "difficult national pasts"—such as a country's complicity in the Holocaust or its legacy of colonialism? Are immigrants asked to share such critical attitudes with regard to the majority's national past? Or are they to make the "politics of regret" meaningful for the histories and national narratives of their (or their parents," let's say) countries of origin? It would be wrong to think that a critical engagement with the host country's difficult past would necessarily indicate liberal nationalism, such that everyone now revises and furthers the same national identity or project. Nor is it realistic to think that all difficult pasts can easily yield "universal lessons," so that national specificity is somehow avoided altogether—a difficulty to which I'll return in the next chapter. My sense here is that a stress on "universal lessons," where plausible, would point toward constitutional patriotism, as would a more inclusive approach that focuses on "entangled histories" or *histoires croisées*. The latter could be a particularly strong sign that political cultures are becoming more porous, in a process of mutual opening. However, to address such questions more meaningfully, we clearly need to leave the focus on individual polities behind. Let me therefore shift to considering a continent whose histories are without a doubt deeply entangled, and yet can also present one of the most credible claims to have achieved some kind of mutual opening of polities.

Three

A EUROPEAN CONSTITUTIONAL PATRIOTISM?

On Memory, Militancy, and Morality

> Few things have played a more fatal part in the history of human thought and action than great imaginative analogies from one sphere, in which a particular principle is applicable and valid, to other provinces, where its effect may be exciting and transforming, but where its consequences may be fallacious in theory and ruinous in practice.
> —Isaiah Berlin, "European Unity and Its Vicissitudes"

O VER the years a number of politicians and intellectuals have openly expressed the wish to see the formation of a constitutional patriotism centered on the European Union (EU). To understand the reasons behind this wish (or, in the eyes of some, wishful thinking) I'll start this chapter with a few words about the development of the EU, at once an "unidentified political object" and, at least for some observers, "an empire in many respects the most interesting in the world."[1]

From its inception in the 1950s, European integration has been a political end pursued by economic and administrative means. The idea of small (economic) steps and grand (political) effects was designed to bring about lasting peace and prosperity on a ravaged continent, or at least the western half of it: apparently low-level technocratic measures, initially hardly visible for the peoples in the founding countries, were supposed eventually to "spill over" into high politics. In retrospect, the process often appeared like integration by stealth.

What became known as "the European Community" soon moved beyond a classic association of nation-states. European Community law began to have supremacy over national laws and to acquire direct effect in member states. Both doctrines were based on decisions by the European Court of Justice, which more or less bootstrapped itself into a position of extraordinary judicial power—and was accepted as possessing that power by national courts. When the Community gathered importance (and additional members), the unelected bodies of the European Commission, Court, and Council of Ministers were in 1979 complemented by the first direct elections to a supranational institution, the European Parliament. At this stage, the European Community had already acquired a genuine system of supranational, quasi-federal law and a basic—albeit not very far-reaching—"economic constitution."[2] But it was neither a state, nor did it seem any longer to be a mere international organization based on one-off treaties.

For decades, the Community appeared to enjoy what political scientists call "diffuse" support—as opposed to specific, actively expressed support. Like the British with their empire, Western Europeans seemed to have acquired a Community in moments of absent-mindedness—they didn't think much about it, and, when they did, they went along with it. In the 1980s and 1990s, however, the process of European integration gathered momentum—and encountered genuine doubts and even outright resistance on the part of various populations. Especially with the negotiations of the Maastricht Treaty in late 1991, which introduced a common currency, and the completion of the Single European Market (that is, the common market) in 1992, "Europe" acquired unprecedented salience in (for the most part, national) public debates. In June 1992 Denmark famously (and, from the point of view of the Community, scandalously) voted against the Maastricht Treaty; a few months later, French citizens only adopted it by the narrowest of margins. In short, "Europe" had come to the people or, rather, the peoples of the continent—but the peoples' response was far from enthusiastic.

What was from 1993 known as the European *Union* had gained political visibility not least because its *political* purposes had come more sharply into focus. Under the forceful leadership of Commission President Delors European integration had been extended to the project of a common currency, as well as a common Union citizenship (which, however, has remained based on citizenship in a member state—and of which, according to some surveys, around two-thirds of "Euro-citizens" remain entirely unaware). Such economic and political deepening of the Union then also came to be complemented—or, rather, in the eyes of most observers, rivalled—by the prospect of enlarging it to the newly democratized countries in Central and Eastern Europe. The picture was further complicated by the emergence of a "variable geometry" in the western half of the continent: EU countries were no longer marching in step to an "ever closer Union";

instead, some countries were forging ahead with ambitious plans like the Euro, while others reserved the right to "opt out" of certain agreements. Yet, the new method of multiple speeds also multiplied the concerns about the end-point of integration—what is sometimes, in a slightly unfortunate phrase, known as "Europe's finality," or *finalité*. Consequently, what the lawyers had long described as Europe's de facto constitution increasingly seemed to fit Samuel Pufendorf's famous description of the Holy Roman Empire: *simile monstro*—that is, a monstrosity, incomprehensible to any ordinary citizen, and probably to quite a number of bureaucrats and politicians as well.

In short, the legitimacy of European integration has been increasingly contested. Both those sympathetic to integration and those opposed to the process of achieving "ever closer union" have argued that the limits of the so-called *méthode Monnet*—that is, in the manner of one of the founding fathers of the Community, Jean Monnet, and shorthand for integration by stealth—have been reached; apparently, what founding fathers of the Community such as Robert Schuman had described as "practical achievements calling for real solidarity" are no longer enough. The same goes for the hope of Walter Hallstein, the first president of the European Commission, that something he called *Sachlogik* [literally, the "logic inherent in things themselves"] would lead to a "psychological chain reaction of integration." No wonder, then, that the apocryphal words "If I had to do it all again, I would start with culture" came to be attributed to none other than Monnet.

However, "European identity"—today a thoroughly clichéd topic—had preoccupied the architects of the Union long before the crises beginning in the early 1990s. As early as 1973, the then Community of nine issued an official "Declaration on European Identity." The "Eurobarometer" surveys regularly measure the "identification" of Europeans with their Union—although it often appears more like a Eurothermometer, checking whether the continental patient might not relapse into the fever of nationalism. Numerous official and semi-official efforts have been sponsored to write new "European histories," innumerable conferences have been held to engineer "European public spheres"—clearly, the thinking has been along the lines: "We have made Europe. Now we need to make Europeans." Yet declarations of identity have remained at a level where supposedly shared European values hardly differ from those propounded by the United Nations, or regional organizations elsewhere, for that matter. European specificity has remained elusive, and claims for it have inevitably been shadowed by suspicions of Eurocentrism.

Constitutionalism as Pedagogy and as Panacea?

Against the background of such concerns, the idea of a European constitution—and a European constitutional patriotism—was born. Lawyers would insist that the Union has long had a constitution in the formal and functional senses. What has been lacking is anything resembling a single, unified statement enumerating (and thereby also limiting) the competences of the Union, and laying out the fundamental rights of EU citizens. It's what some came to call an "emphatic constitution"—a constitution enacted by "we, the people," clearly based on liberal-democratic principles, sufficiently comprehensible to citizens, and fixed in time as a distinct "constitutional moment."[3] But above all, an emphatic constitution was to be an instrument to gain legitimacy, to "bring Europe closer to the people" (even if, in form, the constitution would turn out to be yet another treaty among member states).

Perhaps this very idea—that of a written, unified constitution as an instrument of creating legitimacy—also explains why the first efforts to enact a European constitution failed. In fact, one might have seen at work what you might call a classic Tocquevillian mechanism: European elites wanted finally something called a "constitution," rather than another international treaty, as had been the custom before, even if the constitution still actually had to take the form of a "constitutional treaty." There was almost a superstitious belief in the magic of the very word "constitution," as if dignifying policy goals and the distribution of competences with all the symbolic paraphernalia of constitution-making would automatically generate citizen support. And perhaps European leaders had taken this "lesson" from the historical crib of the post-war West German experience.

Consequently, a comparatively modest revision of existing treaties and the adoption of a charter of fundamental rights were designated as "our Philadelphia," in the words of the president of the Constitutional Convention, Valéry Giscard d'Estaing. Constitutionalization was about the Union acquiring a kind of public dignity or even "patina" that men and women would recognize from their national experiences of self-government under a constitution; it was approached, for the most part, as a very sophisticated form of *euro-publicité*, or, less polemically put: a form of Euro-pedagogy.[4]

Now, conceptually, state and constitution can be separated; in fact, many academic observers see the de facto "stateless" federal constitution of the EU as its most distinctive feature.[5] But this is not how many politicians framed the issues. It seems that they wanted only the traditional symbols, not the reality of a federal state. Nobody—least of all the smaller member states—saw themselves as part of a project to construct a "United States of Europe" along the model of the United States.

Like the ancien régime, then, European elites were creating expectations that they were neither able nor willing to fulfill. Popular discontent erupted at just the moment when European elites were trying to improve things at least somewhat by having more mechanisms of participation and contestation. But a concatenation of referenda in some nation-states to ratify the constitution brought out the worst demagogy in some national politicians and a not inconsiderable number of citizens, many of whom portrayed the treaty as something that it wasn't. Thus sceptics could feel confirmed in their belief that the prospects for a full-fledged, electoral Euro-democracy that is animated by sophisticated cross-border debates among an informed Euro-citizenry remain very poor indeed.[6]

Now, all this doesn't make questions about the possibility of a European constitution and "European constitutional patriotism" simply go away. It's just a matter of what kind of constitution, or constitutional treaty, does Europe need—if any? What, precisely, would be the object of a "European constitutional patriotism"? What are we to imagine by a "European constitutional culture," if there is such a thing at all? And what kind of stance or disposition can be imagined vis-à-vis such a constitutional culture? Rational endorsement, as the proponents of the

Zwei Reiche doctrine—supranational reason versus national passion—would have it? And should European constitutional patriotism come with the kinds of supplements, perhaps even "dangerous supplements," of particularity that we saw as having played an important role in the German context? Does that not, as I mentioned at the very beginning of this book, conjure up the nightmare that Thomas Mann most famously formulated as "a German Europe" (rather than a "European Germany")? Should the experience of "German constitutional patriotism" be transplanted at all?

Let me, perhaps somewhat counterintuitively, start with the question about supplements. In other words, what about the kinds of supplements of particularity like memory and militancy (which, I argued above, do have a moral connection with constitutional patriotism)—are such supplements even imaginable at the European level?

Mystic Chords of European Memory?

Broadening a European constitutional patriotism to include "mnemonic elements" would require one of two possible processes (or perhaps even both): first, European countries commit themselves to a separate national "working through the past," in the name of shared universal principles. These norms and principles are then in turn reinforced by the concrete confrontation with the failings of "conventional morality" in particular national pasts.

Something of this sort might or might not be happening already. After all, the 1990s saw the rise of what has been called a "politics of regret": national leaders increasingly have assumed collective responsibility for past misdeeds and have engaged in public acts of atonement.[7] Whether this public repudiation of the past constitutes a new form of political legitimacy as such is still very much open to question, but that it is spreading as a type of political claim making can hardly be disputed.

Yet a shared, Europe-wide constitutional patriotism— this is the second possible process—might be more demanding than a series of apparently national instantiations of the politics of regret: it seems that it would have to include "new pasts" for each member. This could mean that Europeans acknowledge the collective memories of other countries, strange as that might sound initially. Or it could mean that "transnational memories" might have to be the basis of a European sense of belonging. On the surface, the first option indeed seems awkward, perhaps even absurd: a national collective *can* take responsibility for its past, much in the way that Jaspers and Habermas had suggested, and even argue about its past in continuous public communication. Yet it is far from clear that nations could—let alone should—argue about *other* nations" pasts. Should the Germans judge France's "Vichy syndrome," that is, the repression of French collaboration with the Nazis after 1945? Why should the French debate the British treatment of the Irish? Are the Spanish in a position to feel sorry for Portuguese colonialism? There is a sense in which one can acknowledge (and even emulate) the success of other countries in coming to terms with their pasts, but one cannot do it for them.

And yet some European countries are actually moving forcefully in the direction of dealing with other nations" pasts. For instance, the French National Assembly passed a resolution that classified (and condemned) the treatment of Armenians during the First World War as genocide. The resolution was approved against the explicit wishes of the French government and even the President (and was to be followed by draft legislation in 2006 that made Armenian genocide–denial a crime punishable by a year's imprisonment and a fine of 45,000 Euros). The point of the initial resolution was officially, and internationally, to recognize the character of the events as "genocide." Defenders of such a resolution argued that the fact of genocide did not depend on recognition or acknowledgment by the national collective of the perpetrators. The fact that *French* politicians had named what had to be named was irrelevant. Shameful truths are not national property, even if their recognition was also to satisfy the political demands of the Armenian minority within France, and, last but not least, to increase the moral capital of French politicians themselves.

It is morally preferable that recognition and acknowledgment become "nationalized," that the actual "intersubjective liabilities" of particular collectives are put in question; clearly, the aim in this case was to prompt an acknowledgment from the Turkish government itself, and then, ideally, a more open debate in Turkish civil society, and, perhaps finally, an official apology. Yet reasoning about consequences was secondary to the acknowledgment of atrocity as such: the fact that nationalists in Turkey might be helped, rather than hindered, by such outside pressure was one, but only one, consideration.[8] There are prudential reasons for refraining from such historical acknowledgments, but at least I can't see genuinely moral ones. Once the character of past events has been admitted, historical truth cannot remain national property. It is another matter to claim that apology—as opposed to recognition or acknowledgment—is a matter only for the collective of the perpetrators.

Secondly, it's not prima facie impossible to "merge" historical memories to some extent or to draw on "transnational memories," and to forge a common political culture in the process of arguing about these pasts. At first sight, this prospect might seem on an equal footing with the well-known nationalist manipulation of memories, or even evoke Orwellian images of the manipulation of individual consciousness. Moreover, it appears to come up against the argument, most powerfully advanced by Avishai Margalit, that only "thick" ethical communities like families and nations have a duty to remember in the first place, while "thin" moral relations (and humanity at large) are not and should not be concerned with memory.[9]

I think one needs to draw a number of distinctions here, and be careful not simply to transfer concepts from individual psychology to the collective. Most importantly, a distinction has to be put in place between collective or national memory, on the one hand, and individual mass memory, on the other.[10] The former refers to "frames" of remembrance, while only the latter designates the memories of participants in actual historical events. And it is collective memory, as a kind of *narrative* that nations or other groups tell about themselves that is subject to moral claims and counter-claims.

In other words, what are at issue are public, collective memories and public claims about these memories—not private, unarticulated, or even involuntary memories. "Memory claims" of the former sort are *always* political in the sense that they demand collective recognition and are aimed at creating legitimacy. They are consciously shaped and reshaped both by "producers" and "consumers" of memory—and they are not a matter of "trauma" and "repression," as false analogies with individual psychology suggest—just as public acknowledgment cannot simply be assumed to lead to private or even collective "healing." They can—and should be—subject to shared public reason, historical scrutiny, and moral argument in a way that individual memories simply are not.

An example of such a recent "transnational memory" might be the collective failing (and shame) over Bosnia in the early to mid-1990s. An "overlapping moral consensus" seems to have emerged that Europe betrayed its own liberal ideals in its reluctance to intervene. Of course, it's difficult here to draw a line between European and international, but given how fervently representatives of the EU claimed at the beginning of the Yugoslav Wars that this was "Europe's hour," the responsibility for successive failures would have to be attributed to the EU at least as much as the UN or individual countries.

Moreover, one shouldn't exaggerate the artificiality of such a transnational perspective: after all, so many national history and memory already are inextricably bound up each with the other; a fact brilliantly symbolized in Emir Kusturica's film *Underground*, where vast tunnels connect not just European cities, but also different historical periods: underneath an allegedly "New Europe," it seems, various pasts remain linked in a way that, above ground, appears to be covered by historical amnesia, but in fact allows for shortcuts in political argument by historical allusion and analogy. But genuinely "entangled histories," or *histoires croisées* by definition require shared and potentially conflicting efforts at historical (and moral) reconstruction. It's against this background that Jean-Marc Ferry, for instance, has suggested a self-critical "opening" of European national memories for one another, as well as attempts to achieve a kind of "overlapping consensus" through civilized conflict and confrontation.[11] To be sure, such a mutual opening is risky and in danger of being hijacked by populist politicians in particular, but, in the best case, it might "de-center" national memories and could contribute to the creation of an "enlarged mentality," as far as thinking about Europe's pasts is concerned.

Not least, the EU itself has always been a kind of monument to the Second World War. It's not simply starry-eyed pro-European rhetoric to say that it was the memory of the War which animated the likes of Robert Schuman, Konrad Adenauer and Alcide de Gasperi; it's also not rhetoric to point out that the likes of Helmut Kohl still pursued a fusion of European interests on the basis of memories of large-scale violence and atrocity. The fact that these memories often remained hidden behind the language of technocracy and economic benefits does not detract from the actual motives of the founders (and subsequent re-founders) of the Union.

In the post-war period, Europeans attempted to develop a language for history which was, so to speak, both monumental and critical. It was about drawing *negative* lessons from the past, and, consequently, building "critical monuments," prima facie an oxymoron (and a fusion of two seemingly incompatible Nietzschean categories), but, in practice, a new potential form of legitimacy.[12] No wonder, then, that some European intellectuals have gone so far as to claim that the impulse "critically to work through the past" is the essence of "European civilization." Alain Finkielkraut, for instance, has argued that if "it is at the expense of his culture that the European individual has conquered, one by one, all his liberties, it is also, and more generally, the critique of tradition which constitutes the spiritual foundation of Europe."[13]

Such rhetoric is always precariously perched between European self-deprecation and Eurocentrism—and one can all too easily turn into the other. There's no point in replacing self-congratulatory national histories with self-congratulatory supranational histories, and some relativization and some reminders are in order. Not least, even the idea of European unification itself has a deeply conflicted history—a history that needs to be remembered especially in order to counter simplistic narratives of European progress against the background of negative national pasts: after all, the last great project of European unification *before* the formation of the European Communities was Hitler's plan for a "New Europe." In fact, attempts at formulating and founding such a "New Europe" are one of the prime examples of a mixing of memories (and guilt) across national boundaries.[14] Many intellectuals and bureaucrats across the continent enthusiastically supported the project, and a whole ideology—which was not simply identical with Nazism—was built around ideas of peace and specific "European values." And it was not least because of this cluster of associations—Hitler, Europe, conquest, and colonialism—that many left-wing intellectuals after 1945 were opposed to the EC. According to the French sociologist Edgar Morin, for instance, it was only through the experience of decolonization that the idea of Europe itself became "purified" for his generation.[15]

Now, some have detected even intimations of what has been called a "Europeanization" of the Holocaust, although at closer inspection it becomes clear that at least British, French, and German views of the Holocaust remain deeply divided—for rather obvious reasons.[16] Nevertheless, a pattern seems to have emerged that individual European nations acknowledge their role in the Holocaust, while at the same time affirming its "universal significance." In France, Italy, and even in Switzerland, Denmark, Sweden as well as Holland, the last decade of the twentieth century saw extensive debates about collaboration, slave labor, and "Nazi Gold." Moreover, after the collapse of Communism, memories of the Second World War were "unfrozen" on both sides of the former Iron Curtain. This is not to say that some pristine, pre-representational memory, free of any political instrumentalization, could suddenly be recovered. But it is to say that collective memories—and, to some degree, even individual memories—were liberated from constraints imposed by the need for state legitimation and friend-enemy thinking associated with the Cold War.

One consequence appears to be that many myths of resistance and purity of the post-war period have been dissolved—which, obviously, is not to claim that guilt or responsibility can ever be distributed equally across the continent. Immediately after the War, nations quickly needed to assert themselves and to find—and legitimize—their role in the global confrontation between East and West. Arguably, European integration has helped Western European countries to gain some distance from their own pasts, as these pasts ceased to serve the particular post-war function as moral foundations of individual nations; integration lessened the need for national self-assertion, for homogeneous narratives of national continuity—and therefore the need to present a morally pristine past.[17]

La hantise du passé is thus no longer a German peculiarity.[18] It might be too much to claim that the Nazi experience as a whole has been "Europeanized," but certainly there is now a common language of guilt, of political entanglements and fateful exclusions. In short, national collective memories have become more heterogeneous and discontinuous, less "mythical," if you like, while free-floating particles of these memories in turn seem to coalesce into a "thin," transnational European memory.

A similar process of "unfreezing" and fragmentation has taken place in Central and East Central Europe. The painful Polish self-interrogation over the massacre at Jedwabne, the bitter debates surrounding Budapest's "House of Terror," and the German-Czech disputes over the Beneš-decrees—these are only a few examples of intense recent historical controversies, in which, often enough, Nazism, Communism, and collaboration were all at stake at once. In each case, history and national identity have been linked more or less directly, and in each case, a European dimension was eventually added to the discussions. For some Central and Eastern European countries set to join the EU, establishing Holocaust memorial days seems to have become almost a test case of their liberal-democratic morality.[19]

Arguably, European integration has helped these processes of critical self-reflection. The prospect of inclusion has made Central and Eastern European politicians and intellectuals *more* willing to question national identities; the security of "belonging to Europe"—even if sometimes on rather unfavorable terms—has also made self-questioning more secure. This also weakens the frequent claim that accession countries do not have traditions of constitutional patriotism, or that, since they have only just regained sovereignty in the name of nationality, they would resent supranational integration (even if they might consent to it as a sheer economic necessity).

And yet, frequently drawing on the history (or, more accurately, histories) of the Holocaust is bound to open the Pandora's Box of problems inevitably associated with historical analogies. James Bryce's judgment that "the chief practical use of history is to deliver us from plausible historical analogies" will not deter politicians, intellectuals, and citizens from rummaging trough the past. But analogical reasoning is likely to have poor results, for reasons rooted in cognitive psychology.[20] If nothing else, they serve to reduce complexity and short-circuit critical reflection for the sake of creating what appears like "instant legitimacy." There is no reason why invoking the Holocaust would not be subject to such problems.

There's also a distinct ethical question about the use of analogies, which has been debated most extensively in connection with "drawing lessons" from the Holocaust: "drawing lessons," as laudable as it might be in the abstract, can be part of a strategy of *consolation*, of deriving a comforting meaning from the past, rather than adopting a more painful strategy of *confrontation* with the past.[21] It is in any case often indeterminate what these lessons would be. As, for instance, Giorgio Agamben and Norman Geras have claimed, the Shoah can also be read as a conclusive refutation of well-meaning universalist morality as its affirmation:[22] Auschwitz was philosophically or "conceptually" devastating, too—and therefore resists any facile appropriation for the sake of reinforcing moral doctrines.[23]

Finally, there's the concern that an emphasis on as momentous (and, in a negative sense, monumental) an event as the Holocaust might shackle constitutional patriotism almost completely to the past, so that remembrance comes at the cost of promoting universalist values in the present. Solidarity is a scarce good in politics, and "anamnestic solidarity" is not unlikely to crowd out present-day solidarity: the sheer enormity of the Holocaust might make it actually more difficult to perceive injustice in the present. As has often been pointed out, the rise of a "politics of regret" has also been associated with a retreat from transformative politics and the replacement of a politics of mass mobilization with a "politics of legal disputation."[24] Some critics have gone so far as to claim that—like neoliberalism—the politics of regret and reparations is, above all, directed against the state, and that it leads to a private cultivation of (or even competition for) victimhood and a juridification of public life, all of which are ultimately apolitical.[25]

Now, these are quasi-empirical predictions which might or might not be accurate. There's no way of showing that "anamnestic solidarity" will drive out other kinds of solidarity, and why it couldn't, rather, make societies as a whole more sensitive to wrongs and instances of open or hidden violence in the present. Also, none of the arguments discussed above suggests that there should be a moral-cum-political *cordon sanitaire* around the Holocaust, as if that were even a possibility. But they should warn against facile analogies, against the complacency of only spending scarce political attention on familiar images, and against misguided "strategies of consolation." After all, even if one holds the view that universally valid insights can be derived from the Holocaust, it does not follow that every universalism needs recourse to the Holocaust to be effective or even fully comprehended.[26] And there is no compelling reason why the experiment of the EU necessarily needs it, either. As Élizabeth Lévy has remarked pointedly, it would be "astonishing if Europe determined its future in response to some 'negationists,' who are fortunately marginal."[27]

But, then, might there not be other memories to be shared and contested across Europe? One readily available answer is memories of colonialism. Almost all Western European countries have histories that are intertwined through imperialism—histories and memories that still profoundly shape the present, as these countries face similar challenges of trying to make immigrants from former colonies "feel at home." The imperative to acknowledge French crimes during and after the Algerian War, for instance, is inseparable from the question of how to open the *République* to its minorities.[28] It's at least debatable, however, whether here past experiences, including ones of moral failure, can yield "universal lessons" in the way it is often claimed about the Holocaust—lessons, for instance, that could be learned by the son of the *harki* as easily as the daughter of the FLN combatant. This challenge, then, also places a particular burden on public reason—that is, on trying to think things through together, keep the past alive by wanting to compare history to memory, and keep arguing about it.[29]

In sum, a strategy of what you might call a conscious "memorialization" of European politics carries significant risks. Even if drawing on different, criss-crossing, and partially conflicting memories is in principle possible, it has to be in itself remembered that European memories are not just divided—they are also divisive. This is not the same point which critics of the "memory industry" have often made—namely, that memories are necessarily of a "liturgical" and non-negotiable character, so that memory becomes quasi-sacred, unquestioned and in fact unquestionable.[30] As I pointed out above, it's not in principle impossible to subject collective memories—as opposed to mass individual memories—to public contestation and public reason.

A Europe that tries to narrate a history about itself ex negativo—with the Holocaust as a "negative foundation myth," as has sometimes been suggested—can easily turn into a monumental enterprise of sentimentalizing the past, and, perversely, deriving consolation for it, while yet remaining politically passive in the present. That is, a shared European public reasoning with respect to its collective pasts and the "admonitory meaning and moral purpose" it might thereby furnish is profoundly desirable: Euro-nation-building through negative memory building is not.[31]

Militancy: "Un-European Activities"?

So if memory is not readily available, or even morally desirable, as a motivational "supplement" to European constitutional patriotism, then the alternative might seem a stronger emphasis on what you might call the "combative supplements" of constitutional patriotism. Almost all EU member states have traditions and provisions of militant democracy, or what Peter Niesen has called "negative republicanism"—that is, mechanisms for defending democracy that refer back to and repudiate *particular* national pasts.[32] Moreover, the European Court of Human Rights has affirmed the idea of militant democracy in reviewing national legal decisions, thereby setting a precedent for the EU.[33] Could there, then, not be an "overlapping consensus" through which European states find cohesion by defining internal limits to political speech and behavior? And is militant democracy not the obvious way of making memory politically relevant for the present?

In a sense, the EU has already had one experience with supranational militancy, and interestingly, not only militancy but also political morality and memory played a role in the decision to sanction the Austria that had included Jörg Haider's Freedom Party in a coalition government in the spring of 2000. Suddenly there seemed to be a determined political will shared by a number of European leaders to show that Europe finds its limits not with any geographical, let alone civilizational, borders, but with a certain kind of politics. Individual democracies enacted bilateral sanctions against Austria, while encouraging their civil societies to "shame" the Austrians. These sanctions were of a particularly (and peculiar) moral character—official representatives of European democracies would deny their Austrian counterparts recognition in diplomatic encounters by refusing handshakes, by leaving the room, and through similar gestures (or lack of same). Memory played an important role in European democracies acting in concert against Austria: it hardly seemed an accident that European leaders took steps against Austria almost immediately after the Stockholm "Holocaust Forum" in January 2000, where they solemnly pledged "collective responsibility."[34] The moralization and memorialization of European politics went hand in hand, as memory was invoked as a motiva-

tional resource for moral action and for renewed identification with universal norms.[35]

Why not, then, build on this example and flesh out an
idea of a proper EU militant democracy? We need to
distinguish two possible scenarios here: one is an EU
member state government actually turning undemo-
cratic or illiberal in a more or less obvious manner—a
case which would require the expulsion of the state from
the Union, and for which, in a sense, no pan-European
idea of militant democracy is required. The other sce-
nario is the rise of antidemocratic parties and movements within member states. Here the principle of sub-
sidiarity would suggest that states are themselves in the
best position to judge how they wish to confront such
parties and movements, and how important a place political toleration ought to have in their political cultures.
Given how difficult it is to predict what results measures
commonly associated with militant democracy might
have, European countries could certainly learn from
each other, and perhaps over time improve the legal-
technical "tool kit" of militant democracy. Brussels
might help this process and act as a kind of "clearing
house," but it must not enter into anything that might
resemble determining "un-European activities."

The matter is different again, however, if one shifts
from state-initiated measures of militant democracy to
civil society. After all, to return to the Austrian example,
anti-Haider protests were also expressed through demonstrations by ordinary citizens in various European countries (and Austria itself, of course), as well as through
more individual measures, such as boycotting Austria for
holidays. Symbolic gestures of this kind were largely attempts at political shaming, of drawing attention to, and

expressing disgust at acts seen as politically shameful. Prima facie, there is much to be said in favor of such shaming, even "transnational shaming," through ordinary citizens, as opposed to politicians or judges exclusively handling the machinery of militant democracy. Politicians, after all, would often be suspected of hypocrisy— that is, of promoting their own popularity or the national interest of their country behind the veil of moral concern. Judges, on the other hand, react more slowly, and, of course, *should* react more slowly, and be constrained by procedural logic. Thus, politicians might be too political, while judges might be not political enough in the case of real anti-democratic challenges. These potential problems are not specific to the European level, but they might be exacerbated once one shifted beyond the framework of a particular nation-state.

The defense of democracy—and the protective and, in particular, the promotional aspects of constitutional patriotism—might, then, in many cases be left to civil society and civic associations within the polity and in other polities, rather than the state as such. Think, for instance, of counter-demonstrations, candlelight processions, and boycotts. Counter-demonstrations in particular have played a large part in civic protests against right-wing violence in Germany and against ETA in Spain. Participants in such demonstrations, one could say, affirm democracy as protective of minorities and even later generations that should be able to benefit from the integrity of ongoing civic learning processes.[36]

Yet, leaving militancy to civil society carries the danger of charging highly vocal but potentially unrepresentative militant minorities with the defense of democracy. Schemes of shaming, like laws, need to be in some sense coherent and predictable; they would have to show that supporters of extreme and anti-democratic forces had somehow betrayed a common understanding about the ethical character of the polity—or, if you like, that these supporters had somehow betrayed that understanding in moments when they lost moral and political "self-possession."[37] In other words, there'd have to be some account of how shaming could demonstrate to citizens that they gave in to base instincts of, say, xenophobia or emotions such as racist anger or even hate—about which in turn they would feel shame as a kind of "meta-emotion."[38] These citizens would then be seen as exposed in their problematic anti-democratic actions and their broader anti-democratic ethos.[39] Demonstrators or counter-demonstrators, on the other hand, would act as "watchers" or "witnesses" in this scheme, and, ideally, the fear of such shame would then hold anti-democratic tendencies in check. Since the main form of support for problematic parties—voting—remains of course secret, one would hope that citizens tempted by anti-democratic movements would eventually come to feel the "imagined gaze of an imagined other."[40]

Thus demonstrations, public displays of indignation, solidarity with the victims of violence, and all other such acts of shaming would have to be the outcome of concerned citizens taking the initiative within the limits of the rule of law; otherwise, shaming could become a matter of "democratic vigilance," self-administered from within civil society, which is not compatible with the rule of law. Only then could one even imagine shame as having a truly "bonding, interactive effect" that is beneficial for democracy as such, and only then might one hope that shamed citizens would engage in attempts at collective "self-improvement."[41]

Yet there remains a more general worry about shaming through civil society, one that is arguably exacerbated beyond the nation-state. As James Q. Whitman has pointed out, political shaming, especially when encouraged, if not organized by governments is easily complicit with a kind of unreflective and emotional crowd politics that might damage the quality of democratic life.[42] This suspicion applies even more at the supranational level. Shaming across borders is easily "nationalized"; it might encourage a politics of national indignation and defensiveness, as was very much the case with Austria in 2000.

Finally, it's worth remembering that the sanctions against Austria were of course, for the most part, judged a failure. Not only were charges of hypocrisy levelled against European leaders (then French President Jacques Chirac in particular, who two years later was confronted with a direct right-wing populist challenger in his own country). There was also the sense that Haider and similar right-wing parties had been misinterpreted, without thereby detracting from their repulsive nature. Sanctions against Austria were often presented as what, in a previous chapter, has been referred to as "negative republicanism"; in other words, they were said to be legitimate not as measures against a more general extremism, but as a means to combat the return of a particular past—namely, the Nazi past. Yet it seemed to strain credulity to argue for an "essential affinity" between the Freedom Party and various European fascist parties in the past, as opposed to the attempt to an understand what was novel, and in many ways truly disturbing, about late twentieth-century populist and xenophobic parties and movements. Establishing

such an affinity would have been the minimum condition
for a party ban or other drastic measures within a particular country subscribing to negative republicanism, where,
in other words, the additional demands for legitimacy
caused by wanting to interfere in *another* country, whose
democratic nature no one denied, did not even apply.
However, given these additional demands for transnational legitimacy, elective affinity would have had to be
proven even more conclusively from such a negative-re-
publican perspective.

Yet there are not only prudential reasons, or reasons
to do with good political judgment, for being cautious
about such militant measures against "internal enemies,"—although the way the sanctions against Austria
backfired should point in the direction of prudence.
First—and this is obviously not specific to "supranational
militant democracy"—there are principled conflicts between the rights of free speech and free association on
the one hand, and the goal of protecting democracy, on
the other. That is to say that there is a genuine clash between the very norms constitutional patriots are supposed to uphold, rather than just tensions between
universalism and the particular contexts in which universalism is instantiated. The only plausible justification for
curtailing democratic experimentalism and collective
learning processes in this manner, it seems, is the claim
that societies have already had ample opportunity to experiment with authoritarian solutions in the past. Everything that needs to be known about the nature and effects
of fascism is already known, you might say.[43] Yet, this justification again puts a particular burden on demonstrating essential affinities between potentially problematic
parties in the present and actual fascist and Nazi move-

ments in the past. Thus, what Niesen has called the "particularist self-restraint of negative republicanism" also limits the applicability of this kind of justification.

So it seems then that there's no obvious place for an affirmation of militant democracy at the EU level. Clearly, the EU excludes the nondemocratic, but below the level of clear-cut deviance from democratic principles it is not obvious what the Union could do, and whether an elaboration of a European militant democracy would yield a strengthening of a European constitutional patriotism. Militancy, significantly more than memory, might turn illiberal, if artificially forced upon member states as part of the construction of a "European identity."

The European Union's Constitutional Morality: A Modest Proposal

Should one not refocus attention, then, on what is actually at the core of constitutional patriotism, in contrast to any supplements of particularity: namely, a constitutional culture centered on universalist liberal-democratic norms and values, refracted and interpreted through particular historical experiences? Clearly, there will be significant overlap, and potentially conflict, between EU member states and the EU itself, as far as the respective "constitutional cultures" are concerned. Is it at all conceivable, then, to identify any kind of "core morality"?

It should be clear by now that we can't simply project a favorite universalist moral theory on the EU as it stands. What Hume thought about human nature, many, whether moral philosophers or not, think about core morality: it's much the same everywhere. It would therefore be peculiar, not to say "Eurocentric," simply to connect the EU with any kind of highly abstract moral theory, or even to declare it a "special area of human hope," as the convention that elaborated the first draft of the Constitutional Treaty suggested. Instead, we might want to ask whether there is a kind of constitutional morality that fits within the constraints of moral universalism and yet is also in some sense *specific* to the EU. We are, if anything, looking for a "moral surplus," you might say, that the Union generates—and if there is no such moral surplus, then of course that should honestly be admitted, too.

One powerful moral justification for European unification was provided as early as 1933 by Julien Benda. In his *Speech to the European Nation*, Benda claimed that

> even an impious Europe will necessarily be less impious than the nation. Because it calls for the devotion of man to a less precise group, less individualized, and consequently less humanly loved, less carnally embraced. The European will inevitably be less attached to Europe than the Frenchman to France or the German to Germany. He will feel much less defined by the soil, less faithful to the land. Even if you make Europe sovereign, the god of immaterialism will smile upon you.[44]

Benda then implored his *confrères* that "intellectuals of all countries, you must be the ones to tell your nations that they are always in the wrong by the single fact that they are nations . . . ."[45] And he went so far as to admonish them: "Plotinus turned red for having a body. You must be the ones who turn red for having a nation."[46]

At least some present-day intellectuals have headed this admonishment. Bernard-Henri Lévy claimed in 2003 that "what I call Europe is what makes me feel a little less French today than I felt yesterday. Europe's greatest merit, in my view, would be to allow a growing number of French people—though the rule also applies, of course, to Germans, Italians and Spaniards—to be able to say, 'I am no longer French, but European of French origin."[47] In the same vein, Pierre Bourdieu, in a talk entitled "The Scientific and Artistic International," appealed to fellow European intellectuals in 1991, "I would like us to become a sort of European Parliament of Culture. European, in the sense that this would be a step forward to a higher level of universalization, which for me would already be better than being French."[48] Benda, often called an *homme sans coeur*, had thought that a unified Europe ought to be a strictly *rationalist* construct to which the poets and all those allegedly enamored with "the concrete" and "the sentimental" would always be opposed; consequently, he demanded that the passions themselves would first have to be rendered ridiculous and even hateful. Ultimately, Benda—and those who've followed his moral lead more or less closely—believed that the moral substance of European nations as such had been compromised by their past belligerence and egotism. In that regard, he resembled some defenders of constitutional patriotism in West Germany who claimed that the nation had been fatally contaminated by being inextricably linked with *National* Socialism. Consequently, every move up to what promised to be more universalist and inclusive forms of belonging was itself morally desirable.

There is also a less dramatic (but perhaps even less persuasive) historical—as opposed to moral—version of this argument. One can hold the view that nations once had a strong moral substance, as they enabled the construction of democratic government by providing the solidarity and substantive equality necessary for the nation-state, which remains the only political form in which large-scale electoral democracy has appeared in modernity. Yet this instrumental value might now simply be exhausted. It's not that the moral substance has been compromised, making nationality in some sense morally questionable and its transcendence a moral imperative; rather, nationality has simply lost its former "ethical significance," as other forms of supranational or post-national democracy become available.

There's a basic confusion at work in all these claims, from Benda's stringent anti-passionate Europe to those telling teleological tales about the loss of ethical significance. There's simply no compelling argument that larger political entities will be more universalist. The Soviet Union was not more universalist or less exclusionary because it covered a larger area of the globe. Nation-states could make themselves more universalist in meaningful ways *without* shifting authority to supranational agencies of government—Europe as, if you like, a concatenation of Canadas. To the extent that universalism commits the state to a defense of human rights and the acknowledgment of the moral equality of co-nationals and foreigners, a policy of generously opening borders would accomplish the desired goals *without* supranationalism.

What, then, about the frequently made claim that the EU guarantees peace, at least among its member states? In other words, the idea, often articulated by EU officials themselves, that "the European Union is the greatest peacemaking project in history"?[49] There is no doubt that ensuring peace was one of the moral intentions behind the project of European integration. And, going a step further, it's also not implausible to see the EU as an anti-imperialist project: it's designed to prevent the hegemonic exercise of power over the continent, as all attempts at European hegemony have always been violent. Spain, France, Germany and, arguably, Russia during the second half of the twentieth century—all these aspiring hegemonic powers and unifiers were defeated during the course of European history. In that sense, the EU could be seen as a peaceful continuation of European peculiarities: the tradition of balance of power, of joint resistance to potentially hegemonic powers, of preserving Europe's internal diversity against attempts at unification by military means—all these, you might say, have been transcended and yet preserved in the EU's peculiar constitutional architecture. A relentless insistence on difference—including a willingness to go as far as secession—marks what you might call the politics of intra-European anti-imperialism. Thus, rather than the Union being a reincarnation of the Holy Roman Empire (or any empire, for that matter), as is often asserted, it's in fact a sophisticated institutional expression of anti-imperialism.

The question, however, is how much moral force such arguments have today, and, not least, how much historical plausibility. There's a rather tenuous connection between the pacification of European nation-states and the project of supranational integration as such, and it would be difficult to establish conclusively that only the European Community offered a solution to Europe's history of conflict and violence—NATO might be a better contender. Moreover, there remains something odd about the frequent rhetoric by European politicians that war would loom in the wake of a weakening, let alone dissolution, of the EU. The discrepancy between war talk and the reality of day-to-day negotiations about milk quotas potentially demoralizes citizens and in fact detracts attention from the real challenges of democratic experimentalism to address concrete problems which, fortunately, tend to fall short of the perils of "war."

Peace is a stronger argument than the supposed fatal compromising of nationality, and it will always resonate at least somewhat across the continent. Many Europeans, I'd submit, are willing critically to reflect on their national histories, but they are probably *not* willing to see them fatally flawed to such an extent that only a rationalist, anti-passionate Europe would save them from themselves. On the other hand, peaceful co-existence, reinforced by interlocking constitutional commitments, will always be part of the Union's "power to attract," without the argument from, and for, peace necessarily translating into a major motivational resource within the EU itself.

Perhaps, then, we should step back from historical justifications altogether. And perhaps we should also step back from a focus on universalist morality, as all kinds of nationally contextualized forms of universalist morality are already present in the EU—the EU, to a significant degree, is itself, after all, a concatenation of more or less constitutionally patriotic countries. Instead, we should do what in some sense is much more obvious: namely, to focus on the peculiar features of the EU itself, and also on the ways in which European constitutionalism might differ from constitutionalism at the state level.

The EU is marked by at least three peculiar characteristics. First, its constitutionalization has so far been an ongoing and open-ended process of deliberation and political struggle. There is nothing intrinsically good about this, as some students of the EU are wont to claim; in other words, there is nothing valuable as such about "keeping the process going" or the character of a political association as a "project"—all will depend on the specific character of the projects, conversations (or entreprises) themselves. Nevertheless, it's important to note the peculiar character of the EU as a polity not based on pre-existing, or, if you like, "prepolitical" solidarities, but on mutually agreed projects and enterprises; it's certainly prima facie true that a European constitutional culture fits the notion of an ongoing *project* much more closely than constitutions at the level of the nation-state. Let that stand as a fact for now, not as a norm or a value.

Second, this process is open not just with regard to its ultimate outcome, but also with regard to its constituents. The EU's normative (and no doubt economic) "power to attract," or what is sometimes also called "the power of induction," translates into two further institutional peculiarities: first, the European constituent power (if there is such a single thing—I'll turn to the question in just a moment) is itself subject to enlargement; second, there is a transnational "normative spillover" beyond the EU's borders. The Union—sometimes directly, sometimes indirectly—reshapes the political cultures of surrounding countries.

Third, the EU is in fact not based on anything that could be conceived as *one* constituent power, or *one* demos (which is true even without further enlargement); rather, it is based on a group of *demoi*. Put simply, European peoples will again and again have to negotiate and decide how much they wish to share in common and how much they wish to keep apart—that is, as long as they are seeking union without ultimate unity or uniformity.[50] Short of complete unity, they might form allegiances around shared projects, based on shared ideals, and in turn develop practices of cooperation, civilized confrontation, and conflict-resolution to serve these shared pursuits. Of course, it's possible to object that the presence of a plurality of *demoi* is an unstable half-way situation between dissolution and a federal state—there is no philosophical or historical argument to refute such scepticism, but the sceptic's essentially *historical* argument is also not in itself a knock-down objection. Just why couldn't the Union be a novel political configuration?

If one wishes to employ the distinction coined by Michael Oakeshott that the EU as a whole is a *civil*—that is, essentially *liberal*—association; and in that civil association, constitutional commitments on behalf of individual member states and the Union as a whole are firmly locked in place; for the most part, "negative freedoms" (not just economic, though) do prevail. But *within* that larger civil association, "entreprise associations" in pursuit of specific policies, projects, and political ideals might take form. What we want to call that larger civil association is an open question: if past meanings are to matter, perhaps "confederal commonwealth" is a good suggestion, not least because "civil association" inevitably conjures up images of Leviathan.

Given this persistent plurality of peoples within the EU, it's at first sight eminently plausible to argue, as Joseph Weiler has done most prominently, that the Union requires a large degree of "constitutional tolerance."[51] It also requires—and ideally enables—a great deal of mutual learning against the background of persistent plurality. Again, this characteristic might not be so obviously an exclusive EU property, but it is at the heart of the European public order in a way that is not the case for member states. The Union's constitutional culture is not so much about "purification" of a public sphere or the "protection" of democracy as such (although both elements are also present in the EU), as it is about taming raw sovereignty, and establishing a politics of compromise, civilized confrontation, and mutual learning.

Here, if not before, advocates of what one might call the "Schmittian imperative" will raise their voices. This imperative, put simply, demands the clear identification of a final locus of authority or of decision making, and, ultimately, the authoritative allocation of a sovereign power, a sovereign deciding, not least, who is to count as friend and who is to count as enemy, and who can call on the lives of individual citizens in the battle against enemies. The EU persistently appears to fail to answer the Hobbesian question *quis iudicabit*—who decides? Power seems permanently dispersed; there are multiple channels of contestation, and numerous procedural resources for calibrating and recalibrating what European nationals want to do in common and what they want to do alone.

There is, in my view, no simple philosophical or legal answer to this Schmittian question. Unless it changes radically and turns itself into a traditional federal nation-state, after all, the Union has *no* single identifiable locus of sovereignty, and it *does* displace "the political" onto the economic and the ethical—just as Carl Schmitt claimed liberalism always would. In other words, it seeks to turn enmity, the possibility of deadly conflict, of killing and being killed, into a matter of peaceful economic competition, and of reasonable debate: an exchange of commodities, on the one hand, and an exchange of arguments, on the other. The EU is not able to call on the individual member of its political community to "die for Brussels";

the ultimate sacrifice is not, and probably will never be, part of the European contract. Call this a "post-political" world, if you wish; call it even if a "post-patriotic" world, if patriotism, in your view, cannot be detached from its association with *dulce et decorum est pro patria mori*.[52]

Of course, this is in a way simply restating the point already made above: the Union is a *liberal* civil association, which is designed to liberate its members from the political, if the political is understood in a Schmittian manner. But the question is: what is supposed to follow from this? *Normatively*, there's nothing missing here: those who associate "political death" and sacrifice with meaning will of course claim that an entity like the EU falls forever short of satisfying a craving for meaning in politics, as well as a craving to have law be "incredibly erotic, political, and dangerous."[53] But that craving itself seems like it's inspired more by aesthetic longing than political judgment.

Now, *factually*, it's true that no post-political association (in the Schmittian sense) can guarantee its own character. That is, enmity cannot be abolished unilaterally; our enemies can still choose us, even if we'd like to be committed to the idea of a world without enmity. This is ultimately also a conceptual point, but that does not mean it's automatically a philosophical Archimedean point, from which an entire normative edifice such as the European Union could be dislodged. If Europe is declared an enemy, Europe will have to declare enmity or defeat, but it might well respond with a specifically European volunteer army whose members have contracted to make the ultimate sacrifice, if necessary. Just as in many nation-states, some will die for Brussels, and a vast majority of citizens will never be asked. This raises questions about justice—that is, the distribution of duties—but they are no different from questions about justice within traditional nation-states.

The Schmittians might say that the Europeans simply got lucky—at least for the moment. And they are probably right. But that doesn't establish a reason why everyone should view the world exclusively *sous l'oeil Schmittien*: it's also a fact that the EU both depends on and furthers a profound cultural-political transformation of sovereignty and the traditional state; the question of *quis iudicabit* is either avoided, peacefully contested and sometimes postponed. There's no guarantee that this transformation cannot be reversed, and, as I said a moment ago, it's not completely within the control of those who have committed to, and benefited from, the taming of the nation-state. But it would not be a sign of political realism, but unrealism, not to recognize what you might call the Great Cultural-Political Transformation, or the Great Taming.[54]

Now, to return to the (at least initial) failure of the Constitutional Treaty for a moment: it might seem that proponents of a post-sovereign EU might have good reasons to feel vindicated by the outcome. After all, if elites had not "oversold" (the advertising language is that of European elites, not mine, though some academics no doubt have also entered the sales business) the EU as a large state—*une grande France*, as it was often put—but explained its real character as a federal entity *without a state*, things might have turned out differently. Europeans could have understood themselves as pursuing constitutional tolerance, rather than constitutional uniformity; as sticking together; and, in crucial respects, remaining apart—as a "People of Others," or a "people of peoples," both real and imagined, for whom the recognition and preservation of difference are to count as supreme values.

While being broadly sympathetic to such a "post-sovereign" reading of the EU, I also want to make three sceptical points about this vision. First, while highlighting important characteristics of the EU as a whole, an overall moral reading of the European constitution cannot immediately apply to individual citizens. What I mean is this: Europeans, in this post-sovereign vision, are said to be ready to accept "the invitation to obey" "in the name of the peoples of Europe," or are ready to engage in mutual recognition on the basis of mutual trust and even mutual identification. They will be invited, in other words, and not forced—and necessarily so, because there is no European state to enforce anything anyway.

The unspoken assumption appears to be that this kind of virtue—a disposition to submit to a higher law and to accept the higher-order rationality of what is propounded "in the name of the peoples of Europe"—is the outcome of a historical learning process. This, though, can easily sound like saying that Europeans have become better human beings, and the entire division into "higher" and "lower" selves tacitly relies on the emotional-national versus rational-supranational doctrine which practically everyone in debates around the EU takes for granted—without much evidence of any kind.

My point is that individual Europeans neither feel "invited to obey" nor in fact obey for the sake of their individual moral emancipation from their lower emotional-national selves. All they do is find themselves in favorable institutional and cultural circumstances that make it easier to live in a liberal civil association and to give what—not to put too fine a point on it—is essentially *losers' con-*

sent for many citizens. In the same vein, the struggle over interpreting liberal-democratic principles to which those inside the Union have committed themselves takes place within existing states *and* beyond them, without any tidy division whereby passion is reserved for one side and reason for the other. This process is simply not captured by the idea of a kind of national self-purification through constitutional discipline, or an implicit teleology of emancipation from lower selves.

The no doubt attractive ideal of mutual recognition and the celebration of difference—this, now, is my second sceptical remark—is in need of some clarification and specificity. Even leaving aside general criticisms of the "politics of recognition," and the peril that what you might call a European "supranational multiculturalism" turns into a kind of "plural monoculturalism," there remain basic questions about the particular agents and objects of "recognition," and its particular justifications.[55]

As has often been said in debates on the concept of recognition, there is a crucial difference between recognition as "cognition," as acknowledgment of something already existing, and recognition as a kind of active celebration of something distinctive and special. The difference could also be put as a difference between recognizing as valid and recognizing as valuable, or between *"recognizing as"* and *"recognizing for."* The notion of "recognizing for" might in turn be further disaggregated: there is the recognition of a special, or even unique, contribution in terms of a shared set of values or goods, a society-wide ideal of ethical life, or *Sittlichkeit*, but then there's also the recognition of claims to special status which might not be framed as a contribution to a preexisting *Sittlichkeit* at all, but are justified with reference to historical injustices.[56]

In a post-sovereign Europe, several types of recognition potentially seem to be at issue. First, in a polity of already constituted democratic polities, the constituent peoples might recognize each other as free and equal and grant each other rights and freedoms. This is essentially the meaning of an overarching European citizenship, and of a Charter of Fundamental Rights (even if these rights only apply between citizens and EU institutions). Second, the constituent peoples could grant each other as *peoples* the right to retain certain differences, or, in Weiler's vocabulary, the right to remain "Other." This is the logic of legal "reservations," "opt-outs," and "cultural exceptions," which of course is separated from protectionism by a very thin line indeed. Nevertheless, it's a right that can be recognized and, in theory, be distributed equally across democratic polities, and that is subject to reflexive constitution-making, un-making, and re-making.

However, the recognition of the right to retain differences could itself become a form of recognition as special, if, for instance, there's a supranational court that determines whether a feature that is supposed to be retained is truly "special" or "distinctive," and not simply, a means to create economic advantage. In this case, the application of the right to Otherness, if you like, would itself be subject to the judgment of a body of "Others."

Then there is the form of recognition to which scholars of the EU have mostly referred when investing the Union's practice of recognition with normative content: mutual recognition of standards and practices among constituted democracies. The question that immediately comes to mind is, however, mutual recognition for the sake of what, precisely? Is it mutual recognition in the name of maximizing diversity, because diversity is itself an important value? Is it to preserve national traditions (irrespective of overall levels of diversity), because these are important sources of meaning—that serve essential needs of individuals? Or is it, more prosaically, to ensure regulatory competition among nation-states which have established a common market? And is such a regulatory competition then in turn justified by the goal of maximizing overall wealth, which in turn might be justified as making a contribution to the well-being of individuals . . .? Or, finally, is it mutual recognition as a demonstration of mutual trust and respect?

There is, in my view, no incontestable ranking of such kinds of recognition, but it should be clear that they are very different in nature; different types of recognition could be justified with reference to quite different values. This makes the need to spell out these justifications all the more urgent so as to avoid the bad faith of, for instance, presenting economic regulatory competition as a case of recognizing and respecting national traditions.[57] Put differently: there's nothing wrong with mutual recognition as a legal instrument in a scheme of mutual economic advantage-seeking, but this is very, in fact easily, recognizably (if I may put it this way) different from a pan-European conversation about criss-crossing, overlapping, or mutually contested cultural traditions and values.

What, then, about the EU as it stands? First, it is important to point out that the Union is, before any recognition among member states can set in, a creator of homogeneity. A polity of polities that is often praised for "transcending sovereignty" is in fact in need of members that have achieved sovereignty in the first place: beyond a general commitment to liberal democracy, those waiting for accession are primarily evaluated for administrative capacity, which, in more old-fashioned language, is a way of asking whether a sovereign can actually implement its will. So the EU is in fact a machine for exporting the European state model; before difference can be recognized, sameness needs to be established. This has hardly remained hidden from those on the receiving end of so-called Europeanization. Witness Orhan Pamuk saying," "Let's love our neighbour, let's love Greece, Iran, Syria. Let's enter the EU and live in peace. But let's not abandon our own thoughts, our own identity, our own personality just because we're worried about 'what the neighbours would say,' just because we should be getting along well with our neighbours."[58] One can of course say that with accession this kind of sameness is then recognized—as in acknowledgd, as in "recognized as." But that's hardly the kind of recognition to which some normative theories refer.

What, too, of mutual recognition, easily the most important form of recognition for different *demoi* within the EU? Empirically, there is little doubt that there has been a significant shift from "top-down harmonization" to mutual recognition, as far as regulation by the Union is concerned.[59] The question, however, is what such mutual recognition is supposed to serve; arguably, it is economic benefits primarily, rather than the preservation of ways of life. Thus, while the exploration of, and engagement with, difference is something that *could* be a major hallmark of the EU, it should probably not be, well, "oversold."

My third sceptical remark—put briefly, as I've already alluded to the point above—concerns the idea that EU constitutionalism ought to be an ongoing conversation, or, if you like, an interminable process. From such a perspective, even what appears like constitutional failure—

the popular rejection of a treaty or an accord—can be turned into part of a much more positive narrative; failure is a prelude to further inclusiveness, to hearing more voices, or hearing the same voices again with a different degree of attentiveness.[60] In this vision, the EU is about a kind of eternal becoming, a permanent Europeanization without ever achieving "Europeanness": a durable form of diverse diversity that is explored, engaged with, and extended. Europe, as two academics put it, is "doing Europe," and what Europe is primarily doing, so we are told, is "organizing diversity."[61]

However, this dichotomy of constitutional closure versus an interminable conversation is a false one. A legitimate constitution will contain avenues of contestation which should enable groups and individuals to reopen fundamental questions, including the norms that govern the process of reopening questions itself. The success of such efforts at reopening is of course not guaranteed, but neither is genuine inclusiveness just because a conversation is continued in some way or other. Citizens also have a reasonable expectation of what EU scholars sometimes refer to as the constitution and European institutions being *lisible*: the political world they inhabit must be "readable" enough to be basically understood, to render expectations stable, to point clearly toward the channels of contestation, but also to allow citizens to take time off politics if they want—even European constitutionalism can take too many evenings. A continuous, self-consciously complex, forever open-ended process will not easily be *lisible* in this way, and might not even meet the criterion that Tom Paine wanted to have applied to constitutions—that they take a "visible form." That is, citizens also have a reasonable expectation for at least temporary constitutional closure, and the pains and pleasures of ordinary, thoroughly non-constitutional moments.

Now where does all this leave constitutional patriotism? Europeans could endorse and also contest the political association that has evolved in the past decades, ideally on the basis of a document that is indeed "readable." At the same time, a conscious endorsement of the particular principles and practices which have evolved in the EU—mutual respect and learning, civilized confrontation, and consensus-fashioning—does not exclude a simultaneous constitutionally patriotic attachment within member states. Mutual learning for the sake of solving particular policy problems and mutual identification over shared projects—rather than "common identity"—could be practices that make for a back-and-forth between the European and national levels.[62] In that sense, the very "multilevel" political architecture of today's Europe might also enable multiple levels of identification and contestation, depending on the particular problem or project in question. Call this, if you like, "supranational democratic experimentalism."

These different kinds of attachments might inform and enrich one another, as in many instances there will be a struggle over the same liberal-democratic principles, their meanings and potential development, and the ways they best fit with an individual nation-state or a common European constitutional culture. Politicians, courts, and, to a lesser extent, citizens can deliberatively engage one another, argue over the "best fits," and, if necessary, find flexible arrangements of participation and abstinence that preserve and further what matters most to them. Individual states cannot be forced to abandon constitutional essentials rooted in their particular histories, but they will remain engaged in a conversation about how other countries, perhaps entire groups of countries, see certain essentials differently. The struggle over principles and practices is thus neither cordoned off at the supranational level; nor does it always have to go all the way down; nor is it, for the most part, all-inclusive or continuous. But that is of course true for nation-states as well.

Now, it would be to evacuate politics from political theory if one did not take into account the possibility of severe constitutional conflict between different levels, and the need to choose among them. Such a thought would indeed give renewed credence to the charge that post-sovereign visions of a perpetually evolving, infinitely varied, and yet harmonious entity called the "European Union" are profoundly apolitical—a charge that can be made entirely without recourse to Schmittian arguments. However, the fact that these kinds of conflicts tend to be contained in a political culture in which only a certain kind of political claim-making is publicly acceptable, and where preserving difference has a certain presumptive validity, reinforces the point that the Union might indeed have produced a range of practices and principles that mark a particular EU constitutional culture. This isn't a guarantee of anything, to be sure, but as a constitutional arrangement, and as a focal point for constitutional patriotism, it is also not so obviously inferior to what we can expect in settled nation-state democracies. Finally, as said before, much of what makes the EU both distinctive and successful can only be sustained, because existing member states remain liberal-democratic. This is a peculiar dynamic that does not supplant nation-states, but continuously transforms them.

But, you might ask, is all this enough? I have essentially taken a different philosophical route from the one followed by Habermas; rather than asking, "how can universalist ideals become effective in existing political entities?" I have asked which moral principles of cooperation we can discover in the process of EU constitutionalization as it has actually unfolded. If labels are necessary—as they always seem to be when exporting goods, philosophical or not—one might describe this as a Hegelian perspective on the EU, a recovery of something that is already there. In a sense, though, these two approaches converge in the end; a post-nationalist political culture will work with and against the background of "what is already there," and a European constitutional patriotism will not just find a foothold in existing practices, but also open possibilities and normative horizons beyond what might have evolved as much by accident as by design.

It's possible, then, to delineate a constitutional morality of the Union, but there is no cause for an uncritical celebration of the EU as a kind of political patchwork without clear lines of authority. Contestability remains essential for ensuing legitimacy for the European project—and contestability depends on citizens not only having the "power to challenge," but also some basic knowledge of where, whom or what to challenge; for that they need what has been called appellate, procedural, and consultative resources.[63] We might then also conclude, at least in a preliminary way, that legitimacy, in the sense here of sustained support for the EU, requires clear points of contestability—again, an argument for a "readable" constitution of one sort or another.

A European constitutional patriotism would find a fixed point in such a constitution, but, more importantly, constitutional patriotism would also be a continuous engagement with its meanings as a project, rather than any static attachment. This is, again, not specific to supranational constitutional patriotism, although the complex, multilevel struggles over meanings renders such a constitutional patriotism in certain ways more demanding than "domestic constitutional patriotism." One could call this sui generis, just as the Union itself is often described, or rather lauded, as sui generis. But that, once more, isn't a good thing in itself, unless one wants to subscribe to what Paul Valéry once called the moderns' *néomanie*.

AFTERWORD

BUT IS IT ENOUGH?

ADVOCATES of constitutional patriotism have to walk a fine line: unlike most of its philosophical competitors, the theory of constitutional patriotism tries to come to terms with the complex nature of contemporary societies. But it denies that social complexity erases the need for liberal democratic attachment. It preserves republican intuitions, in particular about the right of citizens not to be subject to arbitrary power, but it insists that this intuition has to be translated into civic practices for a world in which political attention and political care are scarce resources. Put otherwise, we can't step back into Florence, but we also can't rely on the foil of, let's say, an ideal liberal-nationalist Britain or Canada to render nationalism safe for constitutional democracy.

Contrary to what so many opponents of the concept have claimed, constitutional patriotism *does not* ask men and women to detach themselves completely from national traditions; it also does not have to rely on an unrealistic—and normatively unhelpful—division between the civic and the ethnic. Its purpose is not to create a world in which only one kind of moral psychology remains: that of the exile or the expatriate, let alone the consumer in the global supermarket of cultures (or constitutions, for that matter). Rather, it's supposed to underpin existing, increasingly diverse democracies *and* what we might call "supranational democratic experimentalism." "Underpinning," however, does not imply a simple "identification" with a "moral community," as is often argued; instead, we should envision an ongoing, critical process of attachment, revision, and re-attachment.

Is this enough, though, in the end to add up to a distinctive normative proposal? Is it not slightly rerigged liberal nationalism, or just civic nationalism, under a different flag? Is it perhaps so capacious a concept now that it's actually apolitical? What would be its opposite, if we take seriously Carl Schmitt's injunction that all genuinely political concepts have to contrast with their opposites? Well, for one thing, against the background moral theory I've sketched in the middle part of this essay, it's entirely possible to find oneself confronted with *un*constitutional patriotism—for instance, the kind of nationalism that violates constitutional essentials, and the rights of minorities in particular, in the interest of some purported "national interest." In such situations, the normatively substantive theory of constitutional patriotism would counsel dissent or even civil disobedience, all in the name of the very constitutional essentials that are being violated and the constitutional culture that is being damaged.

I've stressed earlier in this essay that, broadly speaking, constitutional patriotism can be based primarily on an adversarial relationship with a *negative*. That negative might be located in the present, but it could even be located in the past. Now, it's true that "to stand for something is at least implicitly to identify an enemy."[1] But the reverse doesn't follow: we don't need to identify an enemy to stand for something. Constitutional patriotism, in the strong normative sense advocated in this essay, necessarily implies limits to what can count as legitimate politics, and therefore, potentially, militancy. It also suggests a changed attitude toward the past, and therefore a humble form of memory. But it's simply not the case that "identity-building" must begin with *chercher l'ennemi* and militancy, or identifying evil in history. That's why I have been more cautious about supranational memory and militancy, and stressed the potential of a peculiar morality of supranational constitutionalism instead.

One might say that constitutional patriotism is in many ways a strategy of avoidance (or nationalism, above all), and there will always remain at least a tension between universalist norms and the working-through of particular pasts, as well as that between democratic principles and the notion of militancy.[2] It seems to me that constitutional patriotism will be all the more successful the more it argues for argument, rather than for any particular argument about the past; in the same vein, it will be all the more successful the more it is engaged in promoting engagement with those suspected of being democracy's enemies. It's easy to say, but that doesn't mean it shouldn't be said again: in the end, democracies are not just as good as their overcoming of the past or the means at their disposal for democratic self-defense. They are as good as the democrats within them.

Thus constitutional patriotism should be conceived not least as a process of struggle over its meaning—and, partly, its meaning will emerge from the tensions between universality and particularity. Otherwise, if constitutional patriotism is presented as a political identity cast in stone, or as the one and only faithful rendering of what is written on a parchment behind an exhibition glass, it really can be in danger of becoming a civil religion, or even perhaps a kind of McCarthyism.

Tocqueville famously voiced his scepticism about the future of the United States: "I would like to contribute to the faith in human perfectibility, but until men have changed their nature and are completely transformed, I will refuse to believe in the longevity of a government whose task is to hold together forty diverse peoples . . . , to keep them from falling into rivalries, plots, and struggles, and to bring together their independent wills into action for common plans." Has the European Union "completely transformed" the "nature" of men (and women)? Perhaps to such an extent that they have become, as an astute American observer has put it, "cowardly, greedy, and self-absorbed," without "backbones or firm beliefs."[3]

Those seeking to remedy Euro-apathy have often sounded as if the only way forward was to whip up some (largely unspecified) Euro-passions. Most of their proposals have firmly remained within the political (and, especially, adversarial) logic inscribed in the nation-state: they assume that there is an unchanging moral psychology or structure of motivations for political agency required by democratic politics, and by polity-building in particular. Unquestioned loyalty and the passionate pursuit of political ideals are often held to be central parts of that psychology—or, as Burke put it, "no cold relation is a zealous citizen." Even for the most uncompromising rationalists and universalists it appears practically inconceivable fully to leave this logic and its attendant psychology behind. Julien Benda, for instance, the great advocate of "cold relations," in the end seemed to lose his nerve when he advised his fellow intellectuals: "It's a matter of opposing to nationalist pragmatism another pragmatism, to the idols other idols, to myths other myths, to this mystique another mystique." And he went on to define the task of intellectuals with the words: "to make gods." Thus, he finally had to admit that "you will only vanquish nationalist passion with another passion. This could be the passion of reason. But the passion of reason is a passion, and wholly another thing than reason."[4]

The EU might provide an escape from this logic of substituting one passion for another, one absolute attachment for another, one political identity for another. It needs to avoid strategies of replacement (or redirection), in which national passions are simply replaced with "European passions," and attachment is redirected toward a European nation or constitution.[5] That would appear to point to a strategy of relativization, through which passion is somehow weakened altogether, and through which patriotism is pulled away from the adversarial toward rational "achievement"—giving rise to the specter of a *"parvenu* Europe" trying to escape its problematic pasts altogether.[6] The real challenge, however, is to find a form of political attachment that makes room for *both* passion and scepticism, that allows men and women to struggle for the best interpretations of the political principles they hold dear at various levels, and with various configurations, or, if you like, "variable geometries," of reason and passion.

On this view, nation-states remain indispensable, even if they cannot provide a model for how the Union itself ought to be shaped.[7] In the same vein, liberal forms of allegiance to nation-states are not superseded, but complemented by a European constitutional patriotism.

However, "complementing" is perhaps the wrong word, as it suggests a notion of "identity" as more or less a box of bricks. Jürgen Habermas has demanded that Europeans ought to "build another (European) storey" to their national identities, or enlarge them with a "European dimension." But the European self is not a house with a beautiful terrace on which one breathes freer cosmopolitan air while nationalist demons remain buried in the basement. Perhaps it rather resembles a Frank Gehry or Daniel Libeskind building.

Now, it would be naïve, and in fact an insult, to those outside the Union to extol the revision and even relativization of attachment—without relativizing that relativization. A Ukrainian lining up at the Polish border, a Moroccan picked up from a rickety boot off the Canary Islands, or a Nigerian engaged in *attaquer les grillages*—that is, climbing the fences that surround the Spanish exclaves in North Africa—is deemed to have only *one* relevant identity, no matter what his or her wishes for reflective civic attachment to the EU might be. This reality no doubt relativizes the EU experiment itself. But it does not automatically detract from the fact that something new has emerged on the old continent, something that could eventually serve as a model for other parts of the world. This is not Eurocentrism, but a non-patronizing hope for the kind of non-coercive, "normative spillover" described earlier in this essay.

Here, constitutional patriotism as a crucial part of a conception of critical citizenship might also serve as a model: constitutional patriots are always entitled to demand more of their constitutional cultures, to contest, to turn up the "blast" of critical opinion against the political system. At the limit, there is the possibility of civil disobedience in the name of constitutional essentials.[8] In times when adversarial self-definitions and demands for unconditional loyalty have come to dominate the politics of many countries both inside and outside the EU, constitutional patriotism serves as a reminder that modes of self-critical belonging *are* conceivable, without thereby weakening a polity. It casts doubt on the anti-doubt idea that "the relentless reflexivity of modern democratic life" would necessarily undermine political agency.[9] On the contrary, it claims that a process involving both critical reflection and complex emotional attachment can strengthen it. This, at any rate, is the promise—and for some, perhaps, the peril—of constitutional patriotism.

ACKNOWLEDGMENTS

ACKNOWLEDGMENTS in academic books have long since turned into a peculiar art form: part confessional, part *captatio benevolentiae*, but also profession of loyalty, and passionate expressions of attachments to the particular, whether individuals or institutions. Like the common languages of patriotism, they can easily ring hollow, as the stock phrases of "I've incurred many debts along the way" and the like come tumbling down the pages. But as with these other languages, we ought perhaps to assume such legacies and refashion them to bring out what is real and valuable in them. Here's an attempt.

This essay was first conceived, and some of the general ideas were sketched out, at Harvard's Center for European Studies, only to be expanded and comprehensively reworked in other, equally congenial settings: All Souls College, Oxford; the European Studies Centre at St. Antony's College, Oxford; and the Department of Politics, Princeton University. While we can't step back into fifteenth-century Florence, we can at least live closer to its remains, and so I'm also grateful to the European University Institute, Florence, where the book was finished.

Many friends and colleagues have taken the time and effort to react to the ideas and often incoherent intuitions, and I'm especially thankful for the healthily sceptical voices that have greeted the manuscript over the years: those of Timothy Garton Ash, Mark Lilla, and Steven Lukes in particular, who helped me to rethink some of the main assumptions and arguments. As in the past,

Erika Kiss also challenged and supported me with a unique blend of scepticism and passion, and at least tried to prevent me from writing a triumphant little textbook for a *parvenu* Europe.

Especially warm thanks to four scholars who read the entire manuscript at a crucial stage and offered invaluable suggestions: Josh Cohen, Patrick Gavigan, Glyn Morgan, and Kalypso Nicolaïdis. Others were kind enough to offer comments on individual chapters and articles, parts of which eventually found their way into the book: David Abraham, Xabier Arzoz, W. James Booth, Carlos Closa, Jerry Cohen, Amanda Dickins, Rainer Forst, Oliver Gerstenberg, Christian Joerges, Chimène Keitner, Peter A. Kraus, Justine Lacroix, Paul Magnette, Peter Niesen, Jeff Olick, Emre Ozcan, Alan Patten, Peter Pulzer, and Helder de Schutter. I am also grateful to participants in the spring 2006 workshop on "Constitutional Patriotism" held under the auspices of the Law and Public Affairs Program at Princeton, and especially to Kim Lane Scheppele for co-organizing this event with me, as well as for her generosity in sharing her knowledge of comparative constitutionalism.

Individual chapters and parts of the argument were also presented at Harvard, at the Oxford Political Theory Conference, in Michael Freeden's seminar on Political Ideologies at Oxford, at Cambridge, the University of Michigan Law School, the Free University in Brussels, Princeton, the European University Institute, and the EHESS, Paris. I am grateful to the audiences at all these institutions.

Finally, special thanks go to Ian Malcolm, for outstanding editorial work, as much as for subtle forms of support and encouragement over the years, and, above all, patience.

Sections of the book have previously been published as parts of articles; I am indebted to the editors of the following journals and magazines for permission to use these materials here: the *Boston Review, Constellations, Contemporary Political Theory, Critical Review of International Social and Political Philosophy, Dissent,* and the *European Journal of Political Theory.* A number of phrases in chapters 1 and 3 made their first appearance in my books *Another Country* and *A Dangerous Mind,* and in my introduction to the edited volume, *Memory and Power in Post-War Europe.*

This book is for my father.

NOTES

INTRODUCTION

1. Herman Finer, quoted in András Sajó, *Limiting Government: An Introduction to Constitutionalism* (Budapest: CEU Press, 1999), 2.

2. George Kateb, "Is Patriotism a Mistake?", *Social Research* 67 (Winter 2000): 901–24.

3. Alasdair MacIntyre, *Is Patriotism a Virtue?* (Lawrence: University Press of Kansas), 15.

4. Martha Nussbaum et al., *For Love of Country: Debating the Limits of Patriotism*, ed. Joshua Cohen (Boston: Beacon Press, 1996). This echoes Martin Luther King, Jr.'s saying: "A genuine revolution of values means in the final analysis that our loyalties must become ecumenical rather than sectional. Every nation must now develop an overriding loyalty to mankind as a whole in order to preserve the best in their individual societies."

5. Justine Lacroix, "For a European Constitutional Patriotism," *Political Studies*, 50 (2002): 944–58.

6. Michael Walzer, *Spheres of Justice: A Defence of Pluralism and Equality* (Oxford: Blackwell, 1994).

7. Lacroix, "For a European Constitutional Patriotism."

8. "Reis ul-ulema Mustafa Ceric, Oberhaupt der bosnischen Muslime, über den Islam, Europa und Bosnien-Hercegovina," *Frankfurter Allgemeine Zeitung*, January 4, 2006.

9. Or, as Jeremy A. Rabkin puts it, "National pride is controversial in Germany and seems to be discouraged elsewhere in Europe in order to make union with Germany work smoothly" (Rabkin, *Law without Nations? Why Constitutional Government Requires Sovereign States* [Princeton: Princeton University Press, 2005], 250).

10. See, for instance, Anatol Lieven, *America Right or Wrong: An Anatomy of American Nationalism* (London: HarperCollins, 2004), esp. 48–87.

11. See also Seyla Benhabib, *The Rights of Others* (Cambridge: Cambridge University Press, 2004).

12. Todd Gitlin, *The Intellectuals and the Flag* (New York: Columbia University Press, 2006), 131.

13. Patchen Markell, "Making Affect Safe for Democracy? On 'Constitutional Patriotism,'" *Political Theory* 28 (2000): 38–53.

14. For the idea of normative dependence, see Rainer Forst, *Toleranz im Kouflikt: Geschichte, Gehalt und Gegenwart eines umstrittenen Begriffs* (Frankfurt/Main: Suhrkamp, 2003), 48–52. I am much indebted to discussions with Rainer Forst on this point.

15. Markell, "Making Affect Safe for Democracy?"

16. David Miller, *On Nationality* (Oxford: Oxford University Press, 1995).

17. Andrew Oldenquist, "Loyalties," *Journal of Philosophy* 79 (1982): 173–93.

ONE: A Brief History of Constitutional Patriotism

1. Carl Schmitt, *Der Hüter der Verfassung* (Tübingen: Mohr, 1931).

2. The following draws heavily on Jan-Werner Müller, *Another Country: German Intellectuals, Unification and National Identity* (London and New Haven: Yale University Press, 2000).

3. Karl Jaspers, *Die Schuldfrage: Ein Beitrag zur deutschen Frage* (Zurich: Artemis, 1946), 10–14.

4. Anson Rabinbach, "The German as Pariah: Karl Jaspers' The Question of German Guilt," *In the Shadow of Catastrophe: German Intellectuals between Enlightenment and Apocalypse* (Berkeley: University of California Press, 1997), 129–65; here 138.

5. *Hannah Arendt-Karl Jaspers-Briefwechsel 1926–1969*, ed. Lotte Köhler and Hans Saner (Munich: Piper, 1985), 82 and 93.

6. Jaspers, *Die Schuldfrage*, 17.

7. Kurt Salamun, *Karl Jaspers* (Munich: C. H. Beck, 1985), 105.

8. See in particular Rudolf Smend, "Verfassung und Verfassungsrecht [1928]," in *Staatsrechtliche Abhandlungen und andere Aufsätze* (Berlin: Duncker and Humblot, 1994), 119–276, as well as "Integrationslehre," in ibid., 475–81.

9. Dieter Grimm, "Das Grundgesetz nach 50 Jahren," *Die Verfassung und die Politik: Einsprüche in Störfällen* (Munich: C. H. Beck, 2001), 295–324; here 296–98.

10. Dolf Sternberger, "Verfassungspatriotismus," *Frankfurter Allgemeine Zeitung*, May 23, 1979.

11. See also Claudia Kinkela, *Die Rehabilitierung des Bürgerlichen im Werk Dolf Sternbergers* (Würzburg: Königshausen & Neumann, 2001), 285–96.

12. Dolf Sternberger, *Staatsfreundschaft [Schriften IV]* (Frankfurt/Main: Suhrkamp, 1980). See also Hans Lietzmann, " 'Verfassunspatriotismus' und 'Civil Society': Eine Grundlage für Politik in Deutschland?" in Rüdiger Voigt, ed., *Abschied vom Staat—Rückkehr zum Staat?* (Baden-Baden: Nomos, 1993), 205–27; here 207–10.

13. See also András Sajó, ed., *Militant Democracy* (Utrecht: Eleven International, 2004).

14. Dolf Sternberger, "Böll, der Staat und die Gnade," *Frankfurter Allgemeine Zeitung*, February 2, 1972.

15. Karl Loewenstein, "Militant Democracy and Fundamental Rights I," *American Political Science Review* 31 (1937): 417–32.

16. Ibid., 424.

17. Karl Loewenstein, "Militant Democracy and Fundamental Rights II," *American Political Science Review* 31 (1937): 638–58; here 647.

18. Ibid., 656–57.

19. Ulrich K. Preuss, "Political Order and Democracy: Carl Schmitt and His Influence," in Chantal Mouffe, *The Challenge of Carl Schmitt* (London: Verso, 1999), 155–79.

20. Peter Niesen, "Anti-Extremism, Negative Republicanism, Civic Society: Three Paradigms for Banning Political Parties," in Shlomo Avineri and Zeev Sternhell, eds., *Europe's Century of Discontent: The Legacies of Fascism, Nazism and Communism* (Jerusalem: Magnes Press, 2003), 249–68.

21. This sense of "caring" might best capture the particular form of attachment Sternberger was driving at. See Harry G. Frankfurt, "On caring," in idem, *Necessity, Volition, and Love* (Cambridge: Cambridge University Press, 1999), 155–80.

22. For this distinction between belonging and achievement, see also Avishai Margalit, "The Moral Psychology of Nationalism," in Robert McKim and Jeff McMahan, eds., *The Morality of Nationalism* (New York: Oxford University Press, 1997), 74–87.

23. See also Attracta Ingram, "Constitutional Patriotism," *Philosophy and Social Criticism* 22, no. 6 (1996): 1–18; here 15.

24. Which is *not* to say that every patriotism is ultimately ethnic qua particular—as Habermas's conception shows. The difference is the kind of particularity, not the degree of universalism contained in the conception of constitutional patriotism.

25. On the historians' dispute, see Charles S. Maier, *The Unmasterable Past: History, Holocaust, and German National Identity* (Cambridge, Mass.: Harvard University Press, 1988) and Richard J. Evans, *In Hitler's Shadow: West German Historians and the Attempt to Escape from the Nazi Past* (London: I. B. Tauris, 1989).

26. For a subtle critique of such "Kohlbergian triumphs," see Kwame Anthony Appiah, *The Ethics of Identity* (Princeton: Princeton University Press, 2005), 220.

27. For the following, see in particular Jürgen Habermas, "Können komplexe Gesellschaften eine vernünftige Identität ausbilden?" in idem, *Zur Rekonstruktion des Historischen Materialismus* (Frankfurt/Main: Suhrkamp, 1976), 92–126.

28. See also Charles Larmore, *The Morals of Modernity* (Cambridge: Cambridge University Press, 1996).

29. Ciaran Cronin, "Democracy and Collective Identity: In Defence of Constitutional Patriotism," *European Journal of Philosophy* 11, no. 1 (2003): 1–28; here 9.

30. Pablo de Greiff, "Habermas on Nationalism and Cosmopolitanism," *Ratio Juris* 15 (2002): 418–38; here 431.

31. Jürgen Habermas, "Grenzen des Neohistorismus," in idem, *Die nachholende Revolution* (Frankfurt/Main: Suhrkamp, 1990), 149–56; here 152.

32. Ibid.

33. Habermas, *Die nachholende Revolution*, 150.

34. See also Melissa Williams, *Voice, Trust, and Memory: Marginalized Groups and the Failings of Liberal Representation* (Princeton: Princeton University Press, 1998), 177–78.

35. Jürgen Habermas, "Historical Consciousness and Post-Traditional Identity: The Federal Republic's Orientation to the West," in idem, *The New Conservatism: Cultural Criticism and the Historians' Debate*, ed. and trans. Shierry Weber Nicholsen (Cambridge, Mass.: MIT Press, 1989), 249–67.

36. For an excellent argument against such "thick social unity," see Jonathan Allen, "Balancing Justice and Social Unity: Political Theory and the Idea of a Truth and Reconciliation Commission," *University of Toronto Law Journal* 49 (1999): 315–53.

37. Habermas, "Historical Consciousness and Post-Traditional Identity."

38. George Fletcher, building on Harry Frankfurt's distinction between first- and second-order volitions, has made a convincing case for the importance of cultural influence in failing to correct problematic first-order volitions. However, it remains unclear to me how this influence establishes "collective guilt." In my view, the participation of nonperpetrators in upholding cultural structures that might have facilitated crimes establishes a responsibility critically to reflect and revise, as outlined earlier in this chapter. See George P. Fletcher, *Romantics*

at War: Glory and Guilt in the Age of Terrorism (Princeton: Princeton University Press, 2002).

39. Habermas, *New Conservatism*, 233.

40. Roger Scruton, "In Defence of the Nation," in J.C.D. Clark, ed., *Ideas and Politics in Modern Britain* (London: Macmillan, 1990), 53–86; here 75.

41. Cronin, "Democracy and Collective Identity," 14, and Markell, "On 'Constitutional Patriotism.' "

42. Ambivalence also came to characterize the attitude of many intellectuals to constitutional patriotism itself. In fact, in many West German discussions of constitutional patriotism, there remained a fundamental tension. On the one hand, constitutional patriotism was understood as being congruent with moral universalism. It was then used primarily as a critical standard for existing political practices. Others, however, saw constitutional patriotism primarily as a model of de facto collective identity. Such a collective identity would then necessarily impose certain kinds of "conformity" and even "homogeneity"—which, to be sure, could be negotiable and of a liberal kind. In many instances, some of Habermas's followers and other members of the Left were trying to have both. In other words, they wanted constitutional patriotism as an "antinationalist national identity," but without the exclusionary implications which would necessarily come with any conceptualization of "identity." In short, in many debates, the precise nature and the purpose of constitutional patriotism remained ambiguous.

43. Memory is constitutive for caring, although the relationship does of course not hold the other way round. See Avishai Margalit, *The Ethics of Memory* (Cambridge, Mass.: Harvard University Press, 2002).

44. I owe this phrase to Cécile Laborde.

45. As Christian Joppke has put it, "It is no small irony that Germany, the perpetrator, and Israel, the victim, emerged after World War II as the two countries with the most pronounced systems of ethnic priority immigration" (Joppke, *Immigration*

and the Nation-State: The United States, Germany, and Great Britain [New York: Oxford University Press 1999], 261).

46. See Lawrence Douglas, *The Memory of Judgment: Making Law and History in the Trials of the Holocaust* (New Haven: Yale University Press, 2001), and Eric Stein, "History against Free Speech: The New German Law against the 'Auschwitz'—and Other—'Lies,' " *Michigan Law Review* 85 (1986): 277–324.

47. Michael Ignatieff, *The Warrior's Honour: Ethnic War and the Modern Conscience* (London: Chatto and Windus, 1998), 174.

48. See also Amy Gutman and Dennis Thompson, *Democracy and Disagreement* (Cambridge, Mass.: Harvard University Press, 1996).

49. Martti Koskenniemi, "International Law in Europe: Between Renewal and Tradition," *European Journal of International Law* 16 (2005): 113–24; here 115.

50. See, for instance, Helmut Schelsky, "Über das Staatsbewußtsein," *Die politische Meinung*, 185 (1979): 30–35 and Josef Isensee, "Die Verfassung als Vaterland: Zur Staatsverdrängung der Deutschen," in Armin Mohler, ed., *Wirklichkeit als Tabu?* (Munich: R. Oldenbourg, 1986), 11–35.

51. Martin Walser, "Über Deutschland reden: Ein Bericht," in idem, *Deutsche Sorgen* (Frankfurt/Main: Suhrkamp, 1997), 406–27.

Two: Nations without Qualities?
Toward a Theory of Constitutional Patriotism

1. I don't say much about specific criteria for civil disobedience in this essay, but would point the reader to John Rawls, *A Theory of Justice* (Oxford: Oxford University Press 1973), 363–91, with which I largely agree.

2. Frank I. Michelman, "Morality, Identity and 'Constitutional Patriotism,' " *Ratio Juris* 14 (2001): 253–71.

3. I am indebted to Alan Patten for discussions on this point.

4. Michelman, "Morality," 261.

5. James Tully, "The Unfreedom of the Moderns in relation the ideals of constitutional democracy," *Modern Law Review* 65 (2002): 204–28.

6. For instance, George P. Fletcher, "Constitutional Identity," *Cardozo Law Review* 14 (1993): 737–46. For a somewhat different conception of "constitutional culture," see Peter Häberle, *Verfassungslehre als Kulturwissenschaft* (Berlin: Duncker and Humblot, 1982).

7. See, for instance, Albert O. Hirschman, "Social Conflicts as Pillars of Democratic Market Society," *Political Theory* 22 (1994): 203–18.

8. Jürgen Habermas, "Struggles for Recognition in the Democratic Constitutional State," in idem, *Multiculturalism*, ed. Amy Gutman (Princeton: Princeton University Press, 1994), 107–48; here 135.

9. As Habermas put it, "[T]he interpretation of constitutional history as a learning process is predicated on the nontrivial assumption that later generations will start with the same standards as did the founders. . . . All participants must be able to recognize the project as the *same* throughout history and judge it from the *same* perspective." See Jürgen Habermas. "Constitutional Democracy: A Paradoxical Union of Contradictory Principles?" *Political Theory* 29, no. 6 (2001): 766–81; here 775.

10. See also Ciaran Cronin, "On the Possibility of a Democratic Constitutional Founding: Habermas and Michelman in Dialogue," *Ratio Juris* 19 (2006): 343–69.

11. For an argument that demonstrates the persistence of "ethnic cores" within liberal nationalism, see Arash Abizadeh, "Liberal nationalist versus postnational social integration: on the nation's ethno-cultural particularity and 'concreteness,' " *Nations and Nationalism* 10 (2004): 231–50.

12. Pauline Kleingeld, "Kantian Patriotism," *Philosophy and Public Affairs* 29 (2000): 313–41.

13. Especially as pride generally is unrelated to agency. It does not possess what has been called "action tendencies." See Jon Elster, *Alchemies of the Mind: Rationality and the Emotions* (Cambridge: Cambridge University Press, 1999), 283. Or, as Hume put it, "pride and humility are pure emotions in the soul, unattended with any desire, and not immediately exciting us to action" (David Hume, *A Treatise of Human Nature*, ed. Ernest C. Mossner [London: Penguin, 1985], 414).

14. Passions are not the same as emotions which in turn are not the same as moods. As Philip Fisher has shown in a brilliant book, the modern vocabulary of the emotions is directly opposed to that of the "vehement passions" as almost inherently anti-social. Yet, one of the most interesting dynamics among the passions is one passion "blocking another." And it is perfectly plausible that an account of constitutional patriotism would include a notion of shame, or even anger, blocking other undesirable passions, such as fear. See Philip Fisher, *The Vehement Passions* (Princeton: Princeton University Press, 2002).

15. Elster, *Alchemies of the Mind*, 249–50.

16. "What about heroes and victories for democracy?", one might object. The short answer is that such narratives are available and even necessary. But there are hardly any such narratives which are not also ambivalent in some way, and it is adding this ambivalence that makes the difference for constitutional patriotism. One might remember Benjamin's dictum in this context that there is no object of culture which is not at the same time an object of barbarism.

17. Cronin, "Democracy and Collective Identity," 19.

18. George P. Fletcher, *Loyalty: An Essay on the Morality of Relationships* (New York: Oxford University Press, 1993).

19. Ibid., 63.

20. Ibid., 64.

21. Joseph Raz, *Value, Respect and Attachment* (Cambridge: Cambridge University Press, 2001), 16.

22. Ibid., 20.

23. Frank I. Michelman, "Integrity-Anxiety?" in Michael Ignatieff, ed., *American Exceptionalism and Human Rights* (Princeton: Princeton University Press, 2005), 241–76.

24. See Rabkin, *Democracy without Nations?*

25. See also Thomas Nagel, "The Problem of Global Justice," *Philosophy and Public Affairs* 33 (2005): 113–47.

26. For the following, compare Bernard Yack, "The Myth of the Civic Nation," *Critical Review* 10 (1996): 193–211.

27. Rogers Brubaker, *Ethnicity without Groups* (Cambridge, Mass.: Harvard University Press, 2004), 5.

28. Yael Tamir, *Liberal Nationalism* (Princeton: Princeton University Press, 1993), 121.

29. J.H.H. Weiler, "Federalism Without Constitutionalism: Europe's *Sonderweg*," in Kalypso Nicolaïdis and Robert Howse, eds., *The Federal Vision: Legitimacy and Levels of Governance in the United States and the European Union* (Oxford: Oxford University Press, 2001), 54–70; here 64.

30. Dora Kostakopoulou, "Thick, Thin and Thinner Patriotisms: Is This All There Is?" *Oxford Journal of Legal Studies* 26, no. 1 (2006): 73–106; here 79 and 83.

31. See Markell, "Making Affect Safe for Democracy?"; Kostakopoulou, "Thick, Thin and Thinner Patriotisms," 74.

32. See also Rogers M. Smith, "The 'American Creed' and Constitutional Theory," *Harvard Law Review* 95, no. 7 (1982): 1691–1702. The resistance to closure and full embodiment could also be more fully theorized with the conceptual tools suggested in Claude Lefort's democratic theory. I thank Helder de Schutter for suggestions on this point.

33. Gans, *The Limits of Nationalism*.

34. Ibid., 7.

35. Ibid., 15.

36. Andrew Vincent, *Nationalism and Particularity* (Cambridge: Cambridge University Press, 2002), 110–35. As Vincent puts it, "Patriotism . . . captures a tragic duality within the state. The state is both a legal abstraction embodying, in the same

moment, a multiplicity of quite brutal powers—whether in the republic, sovereign person or representative constitutional democracy—and moral and religious themes which inspire love and self-sacrifice" (ibid., 133) However, for an ingenuous argument in favor of seeing patriotism as both specifically modern and inevitably ambiguous, see Reinhart Koselleck, "Patriotismus: Gründe und Grenzen eines neuzeitlichen Begriffs," in Robert von Friedeburg, ed., *"Patria" und "Patrioten" vor dem Patriotismus: Pflichten, Rechte, Glauben und die Rekonfigurierung europäischer Gemeinwesen im 17. Jahrhundert* (Wiesbaden: Harrassowitz, 2005), 535–52.

37. Marcel Gauchet, *The Disenchantment of the World: A Political History of Religion*, trans. Oscar Burge (Princeton: Princeton University Press, 1997).

38. Marcel Gauchet, *La condition historique: Entretiens avec François Azouvi et Sylvain Piron* (Paris: Gallimard, 2005), 373.

39. See also Dieter Grimm, "Integration by Constitution," *I-CON* 3, no. 2–3 (2005): 193–208.

40. Hans Vorländer, "Integration durch Verfassung? Die symbolische Bedeutung der Verfassung im politischen Integrationsprozess," in idem., ed., *Integration durch Verfassung* (Wiesbaden: Westdeutscher Verlag, 2002), 9–40; here 21.

41. Michael Schudson, *The Good Citizen: A History of American Civic Life* (Cambridge, Mass.: Harvard University Press, 1998), 203.

42. J.G.A. Pocock, *The Machiavellian Moment: Florentine Political Thought and the Atlantic Republican Tradition*, with a new afterword (Princeton: Princeton University Press, 2003).

43. Vincent, *Nationalism*, 125–35.

44. George Kateb, "Aestheticism and Morality: Their Cooperation and Hostility," *Political Theory* 28, no. 1 (2000): 5–37.

45. Vorländer, "Integration durch Verfassung?" 29.

46. Kostakopoulou, "Thick, Thin and Thinner Patriotisms."

47. Grimm, "Integration by Constitution," 196.

48. Benhabib, *The Rights of Others*.

49. Think of the de facto creation of the *Conseil Français du Culte Musulman* by the French state, and the series of *Islamkonferenzen* initiated by the German Interior Ministry. One might object that these are rather desperate attempts to address challenges of cultural diversity with the tools of old-style European corporatism. However, the reaction from within the French and German Muslim communities have been far too favorable simply to dismiss these efforts as crude state attempts at forcing society to be legible. For subtle discussions of French republicanism's multiple, contested, but also often hard-to-detect adaptations, see Olivier Roy, *La Laïcité face à l'Islam* (Paris: Stock, 2005); Patrick Weil, *La République et sa diversité* (Paris: Seuil, 2005); Riva Kastoryano, ed., *Les Codes de la différence* (Paris: Sciences Po, 2005); and Cécile Laborde, "Secular Philosophy and Muslim Headscarves in Schools," *The Journal of Political Philosophy* 13 (2005): 305–29; for the quasi-official justification of the German *Islamkonferenzen*, see Wolfgang Schäuble, "Muslime in Deutschland," *Frankfurter Allgemeine Zeitung*, September 25, 2006; for the German variant of liberal nationalism in the form of the idea of a *Leitkultur* ("guiding culture"), see Bassam Tibi, "Leitkultur als Wertekonsens—Bilanz einer missglückten deutschen Debatte," *Aus Politik und Zeitgeschichte*, B 1–2 (2001): 23–26.

50. Brubaker, *Ethnicity*, 116–31.

51. Christian Joppke, *Selecting by Origin: Ethnic Migration in the Liberal State* (Cambridge, Mass.: Harvard University Press, 2005).

52. For the perhaps somewhat less obvious example of the Danish case as one of universalism imbued with national and religious particularism, see Per Mouritsen, "The Particular universalism of a Nordic civic nation: Common Values, state religion and Islam in Danish political culture," in Tariq Modood et al. eds., *Multiculturalism, Muslims and Citizenship: A European Approach* (London: Routledge, 2006), 72–93.

53. James Q. Whitman, "The Two Western Cultures of Privacy: Dignity versus Liberty," *Yale Law Journal* 113 (2004): 1151–221.

Three: A European Constitutional Patriotism? On Memory, Military, and Morality

1. The best—and, particularly, the least Euro-nonsense—overview remains Andrew Moravcsik, *The Choice for Europe: Social Purpose and State Power from Messina to Maastricht* (Ithaca: Cornell University Press, 1998).

2. Christian Joerges, *The Law in the Process of Constitutionalizing Europe*, trans. Iain L. Fraser (Florence: EU Working Paper Law No. 2002/4), 4.

3. Mattias Kumm, "Beyond Golf Clubs and the Judicialization of Politics: Why Europe has a Constitution Properly So Called," *American Journal of Comparative Law* 54 (2006): 505–30.

4. Ulrich Haltern, "Pathos and Patina: The Failure and Promise of Constitutionalism in the European Imagination," *European Law Journal* 9, no. 1 (2003): 14–44. To be fair, the constitution on which leaders agreed in 2004 contained important new elements for popular participation and accountability. If they managed to collect a million signatures in a significant number of member states, citizens could ask the European Commission to propose new policies; more powers were confirmed for the European Parliament, the only EU institution directly elected. At the same time, national parliaments were strengthened in their role as "watchdogs" to check that competences reserved for the member states were not silently "creeping" upward to the Union. And finally, there was the requirement to make high-level political deliberations public—arguably the most important achievement for those who see the Union as fundamentally lacking in transparency, and, therefore, also in accountability.

5. But see also Dieter Grimm, "The Constitution in the Process of Denationalization," *Constellations* 12 (2005): 447–63.

6. European elites, rather than spending millions of Euros on taking polls about the Euro-anthem (the "Ode to Joy," for those who care to know), the Euro-motto ("unity in diversity") and the Euro-day (May 9), might have shown the courage of their convictions: they might have held a pan-European referendum on the constitution the same day—one, let's say, the Euro-day. Instead, they seemed to manage to discredit the very word "constitution," at least for the immediate future.

7. See Jeffrey K. Olick and Brenda Coughlin, "The Politics of Regret: Analytical Frames," in John C. Torpey, ed., *Politics and the Past: On Repairing Historical Injustices* (Lanham, Md.: Rowan and Littlefield, 2003), 37–62; Roy L. Brooks, *When Sorry Isn't Enough: The Controversy over Apologies and Reparations for Human Injustice* (New York: NYU Press, 1999); Hermann Lübbe, *"Ich entschuldige mich": Das neue politische Bußritual* (Berlin: Siedler, 2001); Elazar Barkan, *The Guilt of Nations: Restitution and Negotiating Historical Injustices* (New York: Norton, 2000).

8. Mihran Dabag, "Erinnerung ohne Orte: Warum auch Deutschland den Genozid an den Armeniern anerkennen sollte," *Frankfurter Allgemeine Zeitung*, February 9, 2001, and Cem Özdemir, "Langer Gang am Bosporus: Was gegen eine Armenien-Resolution spricht," *Frankfurter Allgemeine Zeitung*, April 5, 2001.

9. Margalit, *The Ethics of Memory*.

10. I adopt this distinction from Timothy Snyder. Of course, the former in many ways frame the latter, but they are not reducible to them, which is the mistake of those who see memory in purely instrumental terms. See Timothy Snyder, "Memory of Sovereignty and Sovereignty over Memory: Poland, Lithuania, and Ukraine, 1939–1999," in Jan-Werner Müller, ed., *Memory and Power in Post-War Europe: Studies in the Presence of the Past* (Cambridge: Cambridge University Press, 2002), 39–58.

11. Jean-Marc Ferry, *La question de l'"État européen* (Paris: Gallimard, 2000), 177.

12. Friedrich Nietzsche, *On the Advantage and Disadvantage of History for Life*, trans. Peter Preuss (Indianapolis: Hackett, 1980).

13. Alain Finkielkraut, *La défaite de la pensée* (Paris: Gallimard, 1987), 143–44.

14. In general, see Mark Mazower, *Dark Continent: Europe's Twentieth Century* (London: Allen Lane, 1998), 141–84, and for the involvement of lawyers and public-law theorists in particular, Christian Joerges and Navraj Singh Ghaleigh, eds., *Darker Legacies of Law in Europe: The Shadow of National Socialism and Fascism over Europe and its Legal Traditions* (Oxford: Hart, 2003).

15. Edgar Morin, *Penser l' Europe* (Paris: Gallimard, 1987), 140–47.

16. Richard J. Evans, "Blitzkrieg und Hakenkreuz," *Frankfurter Rundschau*, September 16, 2000.

17. Michael Jeismann, *Auf Wiedersehen Gestern: Die deutsche Vergangenheit und die Politik von morgen* (Stuttgart: Deutsche Verlags-Anstalt, 2001), 57–58.

18. Ibid., 59.

19. John Reed, "Poland's president seeks to lay his country's war guilt to rest: Sixty years after a massacre of hundreds of Jews by their Catholic neighbours, an official apology will be made," *Financial Times*, July 7, 2001.

20. Yuen Foong Khong, *Analogies at War: Korea, Munich, Dien Bien Phu and the Vietnam Decisions of 1965* (Princeton: Princeton University Press, 1992).

21. Lawrence L. Langer, *Admitting the Holocaust* (New York: Oxford University Press, 1995), 5.

22. See Norman Geras, *The Contract of Mutual Indifference: Political Philosophy after the Holocaust* (London: Verso, 1998). Giorgio Agamben explicitly sees Auschwitz as a refutation of Karl-Otto Apel's and Habermas's discourse ethics, but goes further to claim that "almost none of the ethical principles our age believed it could recognize as valid have stood the decisive test,

that of an *Ethica more Auschwitz demonstrata*" (Agamben, *Remnants of Auschwitz: The Witness and the Archive*, trans. Daniel Heller-Roazen [New York: Zone Books, 1999], 13 and 64–66).

23. Susan Neiman, *Evil in Modern Thought: An Alternative History of Philosophy* (Princeton: Princeton University Press, 2002), 258–81.

24. John C. Torpey, "'Making Whole What Has Been Smashed': Reflections on Reparations," *Journal of Modern History* 73 (2001): 333–58.

25. Ibid.

26. Saul Friedlander, "Introduction," in idem, ed., *Probing the Limits of Representation: Nazism and the "Final Solution"* (Cambridge, Mass.: Harvard University Press, 1992), 1–21; here 19–20.

27. Élisabeth Lévy, *Les Maîtres censeurs: Pour en finir avec la pensée unique* (Paris: Jean-Claude Lattès, 2002), 45.

28. See, for instance, Jacques Barou et al., *Mémoire et integration* (Paris: Syros, 1993).

29. It's often said that even if Europeans could find some kind of consensus about the Holocaust and the moral lessons from the Second World War, such a consensus would in fact exacerbate the problems of integration, as immigrants and their descendants would neither respond to appeals somehow to "feel guilty," nor necessarily share the historical interpretations offered by a majority population. But this is a far too static and, in a sense, sociologically naïve, picture. As, for instance, Ian Buruma has shown in his important essay on the Netherlands, fragments of collective memories of collaboration continue to play an important role in public debates, and are used (or misused) politically by the representatives of Muslims as much as by those who speak in the name of the *autochtoon*. See Ian Buruma, *Murder in Amsterdam: The Death of Theo van Gogh and the Limits of Tolerance* (New York: Penguin, 2006).

30. Charles S. Maier, "A Surfeit of Memory? Reflections on History, Melancholy and Denial," *History and Memory* 5, no. 2 (1993): 136–52.

31. Tony Judt, *Postwar* (New York: Penguin, 2005), 831.

32. See in particular Giovanni Capoccia, *Defending Democracy: Reactions to Extremism in Interwar Europe* (Baltimore: The Johns Hopkins University Press, 2004); for a more general comparison, see Gregory H. Fox and Georg Nolte, "Intolerant Democracies," *Harvard International Law Journal* 36 (1995): 1–70.

33. Sven Eiffler, "Die 'wehrhafte Demokratie' in der Rechtsprechung des Europäischen Gerichtshofs für Menschenrechte," *Kritische Justiz* 36 (2003): 218–25.

34. Michael Jeismann, "Die Weihe: Das Stockholmer Holocaust-Forum," *Frankfurter Allgemeine Zeitung*, January 28, 2000.

35. Dan Diner has probably made this connection most explicitly and coherently. In early 2000 he claimed that the Holocaust was a "negative apotheosis of European history" and could be interpreted as a foundational event for the Union: "From the ethical imperatives of this event a catalogue of values can be deduced, which serve as the basis of political Europe. Racism and xenophobia, which are not identical with antisemitism and Holocaust, but somehow located in their vicinity, are incriminated as fundamentally anti-European dangers" [note, of course, the expression "somehow"] (Diner, "Haider und der Schutzreflex Europas," *Die Welt*, February 26, 2000).

36. Niesen, "Anti-Extremism, Negative Republicanism, Civic Society."

37. J. David Velleman, "The Genesis of Shame," *Philosophy and Public Affairs* 30, no. 1 (2001): 27–52.

38. Elster, *Alchemies of the Mind*, 255.

39. See Bernard Williams, *Shame and Necessity* (Berkeley: University of California Press, 1993), in particular 78–102.

40. Ibid., 82.

41. Ibid., 83, 90.

42. James Q. Whitman, "What Is Wrong with Inflicting Shame Sanctions?" *Yale Law Journal* 107 (1998): 1055–92.

43. Niesen, "Anti-Extremism, Negative Republicanism, Civic Society."

44. Benda, *Discours à la nation européenne*, 126–27.

45. Ibid., 71.

46. Ibid.

47. Bernard-Henri Lévy, "A Passage to Europe: The Continent isn't just on a journey, it is a journey," *Time Europe*, August 25, 2003.

48. Quoted by Alain Finkielkraut, *In the Name of Humanity: Reflections on the Twentieth Century*, trans. Judith Friedlander (London: Pimlico, 2001), 98.

49. See, for instance, "Après EU, le déluge?" *Economist*, July 5, 2003.

50. See Kalypso Nicolaïdis, "Our European Demoi-cracy," in Kalypso Nicolaïdis and Stephen Weatherill, eds., *Whose Europe? National Models and the Constitution of the European Union* (Oxford: Oxford University Press, 2003), 137–52.

51. Weiler, "Federalism without Constitutionalism."

52. Compare Paul W. Kahn, *Putting Liberalism in Its Place* (Princeton: Princeton University Press, 2005).

53. Ulrich Haltern, "On Finality," in Jürgen Bast and Armin von Bogdandy, eds., *European Constitutional Law* (Oxford: Hart, 2006), 727–64; here 732.

54. James Sheehan, "What It Means to Be a State: States and Violence in Twentieth-Century Europe," *Journal of Modern European History* 1, no. 1 (2003): 11–23.

55. Amartya Sen, *Identity and Violence* (New York: Norton, 2006), and Patchen Markell, *Bound by Recognition* (Princeton: Princeton University Press, 2003).

56. Axel Honneth, *Kampf um Anerkennung: Zur moralischen Grammatik sozialer Konflikte* (Frankfurt/Main: Suhrkamp, 1994).

57. Think back to the initial failure of the Treaty Establishing a European Constitution. The debates around the proposed constitution also revealed, among other things, a profound clash between what you might describe as modern and postmodern logics of conflict. French working-class and lower mid-

dle-class anxieties were most effectively stoked by the specter of the "Polish plumber," who would steal over from Poland to fix bidets for a pittance and destroy fine French plumbing craftsmanship. And the problem clearly was not that the French did not want to recognize the plumber in all his Polishness, but rather who was going to get the work. In the face of such anxieties, talk of celebrating diversity and recognizing each other in all one's glorious difference would seem to be at best irrelevant; worse, it might be exemplary of the kind of insults that ruthless cosmopolitans consciously or unconsciously have for those who are forced to stay put.

True, conflicts of recognition and conflicts of distribution can hardly ever be neatly separated. But the problem remains a basic lack of clarity on the part of European elites. All too often, they have "oversold" the Union with, on the one hand, pretentious philosophical rhetoric, and, on the other, by more or less tacitly suggesting that Brussels can solve all the economic problems that nation-states themselves cannot. Again, the rhetoric only exacerbates the sense of frustration when the more basic economic promises aren't kept. For instance, two leading European intellectuals tried to convince citizens once that the essence of Europe somehow consists in "the opening toward the other," "the overcoming of oneself," or even in being together in a "great adventure." These were not Jacques Derrida and Jürgen Habermas, who had tried to define Europe's pecificity at the time of the Iraq War in contrast to the United States; the authors were Jorge Semprún, former Spanish culture minister, and Dominique de Villepin, then French Interior Minister. They had teamed up to offer a definition of nothing less than "European Man" or *L'Homme Européen*, to quote the very title of their jointly authored treatise ("European Man," incidentally, turns out to be a "travelling dream," *un rêve qui voyage*).

Such rhetoric contrasts markedly with the reality of the Union and its—in comparison with nation-states—still rather limited capacities. Because in fact Brussels is not about to open itself to the Other, especially if that other happens to be a Third World farmer, and even if it wanted to, Brussels could not embark on the adventure of reforming the economies of its member states. Still, it's a convenient place for politicians to project false hopes, and, above all, lay the blame for unpopular decisions.

Conversely, of course, increasing the fiscal powers of Brussels would seem the obvious way to redirect national loyalties to the supranational level. One is reminded of the Federalists' advice that "the government of the Union, like that of each State, must be able to address itself immediately to the hopes and fears of individuals; and to attract to its support those passions which have the strongest influence upon the human heart." But generating supranantional loyalties is not an end in itself. And so far, the case remains to be made that a Brussels-directed welfare state would be superior to different, democratically legitimated solutions at the national level. I'm not saying that there couldn't be good arguments for it, or that supranational democratic experimentalism ought to stop short of welfare questions. But a case to be made here needs to start with a picture of different institutional arrangements; it couldn't start with a stipulated European constitutional patriotism—it could only end with it.

58. Orhan Pamuk, "Neighbourhoods," *Eurozine*, October 13, 2006.

59. Giandomenico Majone, *Dilemmas of European Integration: The Ambiguities and Pitfalls of Integration by Stealth* (Oxford: Oxford University Press, 2005).

60. See, for instance, Simone Chambers, "New Constitutionalism: Democracy, Habermas, and Canadian Exceptionalism," Ronald Beiner and Wayne Norman, eds., *Canadian Political Philosophy: Contemporary Reflections* (Toronto: Oxford University Press, 2001), 63–77, and, above all, the work of James Tully.

61. Ulrich Beck and Edgar Grande, *Das kosmopolitische Europa* (Frankfurt/Main: Suhrkamp, 2004), 161 and 137.

62. See also Kalypso Nicolaïdis and Justine Lacroix, "Order and Justice beyond the Nation-State: Europe's Competing Paradigms," Rosemary Foot, John Lewis Gaddis and Andrew Hurrell, eds., *Order and Justice in International Relations* (Oxford: Oxford University Press, 2003), 125–54.

63. Philip Pettit, *A Theory of Freedom: From Psychology to the Politics of Agency* (Cambridge: Polity, 2001), 163–74.

AFTERWORD: But Is It Enough?

1. Kahn, *Putting Liberalism in Its Place*, 235.

2. I am indebted to Steven Lukes on this point.

3. Paul Berman, *Terror and Liberalism* (New York: Norton, 2003), 166.

4. Benda, *Discours à la nation européenne*, 20–21.

5. Markell, "Making Affect Safe for Democracy."

6. J.H.H. Weiler, *Ein christliches Europa: Erkundungsgänge*, trans. Franz Reimer (Salzburg: Anton Pustet, 2004), 20.

7. See also Pierre Manent, *La Raison des Nations: Réflexions sur la démocratie en Europe* (Paris: Gallimard, 2006).

8. Frank I. Michelman, *Brennan and Democracy* (Princeton: Princeton University Press, 1999).

9. Sharon Krause, *Liberalism with Honor* (Cambridge, Mass: Harvard University Press, 2002), 189.

INDEX